MW00787925

No matter where you're from, I'm glad you are my neighbor.

CONTENTS

SECRET
SAN JOSE

A Guide to the Weird, Wonderful, and Obscure

To Saatvik,
   Enjoy uncovering our
      local secrets!

Cassie Kifer

Copyright © 2020, Reedy Press, LLC
All rights reserved.
Reedy Press
PO Box 5131
St. Louis, MO 63139
www.reedypress.com

No part of this publication may be reproduced or transmitted in any form or by any means, electronic or mechanical, including photocopy, recording, or any information storage and retrieval system, without permission in writing from the publisher. Permissions may be sought directly from Reedy Press at the above mailing address or via our website at www.reedypress.com.

We (the publisher and the author) have done our best to provide the most accurate information available when this book was completed. However, we make no warranty, guaranty, or promise about the accuracy, completeness, or currency of the information provided, and we expressly disclaim all warranties, express or implied. Please note that attractions, company names, addresses, websites, and phone numbers are subject to change or closure, and this is outside of our control. We are not responsible for any loss, damage, injury, or inconvenience that may occur due to the use of this book. When exploring new destinations, please do your homework before you go. You are responsible for your own safety and health when using this book.

Library of Congress Control Number: 2020938250

ISBN: 9781681062853

Design by Jill Halpin

All photographs are courtesy of the author unless otherwise noted.

Printed in the United States of America
21 22 23 24 5 4 3 2

ACKNOWLEDGMENTS

There are so many people I want to thank for sharing their stories and their time—these and any that I will invariably forget to name.

Thanks to everyone who shared personal stories and our local history with me. Bill Schroh and History San Jose; Anita Wong Kwock, Chinese Historical and Cultural Project; Karl Soltero, La Raza Historical Society; Joe Feria and Sharlene Mello, Portuguese Historical Museum; Leslie A.G. Dill, architectural historian; Pat Curia, Preservation Action Council of San Jose; Janan Boehme, Winchester Mystery House; Lorraine Katich, Rosicrucian Egyptian Museum; Ranger Lisa Pappanastos and docents from the Santa Clara County Parks & Recreation Department; Chris Boyer from the City of San Jose Parks, Recreation, and Neighborhood Services; Stephanie Jayne, City of San Jose Office of Immigrant Affairs; Paul Lynam, Staff Astronomer, University of California Observatories; Josh Scullen, San Francisco Bay Bird Observatory; Bob Dhillon, Sikh Gurdwara Sahib; Ron Ogi, Wesley United Methodist Church; Trami Nguyen Cron, Chopsticks Alley Art; Yori Seeger, School of Visual Philosophy; Jim Gard, San Jose Printers' Guild; Scott Vanderlip, Tour de Coop; Bess Hernandez-Jones, Hellyer Velodrome; Stephen Borasi, Goodwill of Silicon Valley; Nola Prevost, Prevost Ranch and Gardens; Judy Conner, Bark in the Park; Krazy George Henderson; Further Confusion 2020 and all the furries that talked to me.

Thanks to the Santa Clara Valley Open Space Authority for all you are doing to protect nature in our community, especially the Coyote Valley.

Thanks to the Reedy Press team for letting me feature our great city and Noe Sacoco for connecting me. I owe you a drink!

I'm so grateful to friends who shared their favorite places, helped me uncover stories, and introduced me to people: Susannah Greenwood, author of *100 Things to Do in San Jose Before You Die* (pick up a copy of that book, too!); Jessica Dickinson Goodman and her personal California history library; Layal Nawfal, Cathy Harkness LeMat, Cesar Serrano, Karen and Dan Greenbank, Teri and

Dominique Monbureau, Gurinder Pal Singh, Mandy and Matt Spain, Lance Shoemaker, James Williams, Wil and Michelle Henninger, Alice Adams, Amanda Kraft, Peter Allen, Titus Lin, Shannon Edwards, Rocio Guerrero, Jenny Tsang, and everyone else who has explored our city with me over the years.

Finally, thanks to my family, especially Kevin Adams for his endless support. There is no one I would rather explore our city, and life, with.

INTRODUCTION

Always the underdog while living in the shadow of the much-loved city to our north, San Jose locals understand how many beautiful and surprising treasures hide right here in plain sight. This book is a field guide to our community, highlighting a motley mix of history, arts, culture, food, religion, sports, business, governance, technology, and the natural environment.

Always searching for its place in the sun (even though we already have the best weather in the Bay!), San Jose continually reinvents itself, tearing things down and starting anew. One of the challenges I faced in planning this book was that many fascinating stories no longer have an associated landmark, or if they do, the only thing that remains is a historic plaque on a wall. I apologize for the stories that don't end with a particularly photogenic destination you can visit, but as you will see, that's part of the story here. In this book, I try to peel back the layers and understand the processes and people still influencing who we are today.

I hope you find some places and stories that surprise you in the pages that follow. Please share your thoughts and your own favorite finds with us all on social media using the hashtag #SecretSanJose. I look forward to exploring with you.

A MAMMOTH DISCOVERY

What did the dog get into this time?

When you take your dog out for a walk, you might expect it to sniff out a squirrel or (if it is anything like my dog) the remains of a dead animal or a rotting piece of discarded food. One San Jose dog sniffed up something else entirely—the fossilized remains of a 12,500-year-old mammoth.

In 2005, Roger Castillo and his Labrador Retriever, Jenna, were walking along the Guadalupe River north of the Mineta San Jose Airport when Jenna sniffed at what looked like a bone sticking out of the soil. A geologist from the Santa Clara Valley Water District (who owns the land) and a University of California at Berkeley paleontologist worked together to confirm that these were, in fact, the fossilized tusks of a juvenile Columbian mammoth they named "Lupe." While scientists can't tell whether this particular specimen was male or female, many people usually assume fossils are male, so they chose a traditionally female name. (Also, Lupe, a common nickname for "Guadalupe," was inspired by the river where she was found.)

The Columbian mammoth is now extinct, but they roamed the Santa Clara Valley during the Pleistocene era. After a full excavation of the skull, including teeth, ribs, pelvis, and other assorted bones, it turned out to be the most complete remains of any mammoth ever found in this area.

To honor this important piece of natural history, artists Freyja Bardell and Brian Howe constructed a slightly larger than

Visit the Children's Discovery Museum of San Jose to see "Mammoth Discovery!," an interactive hands-on exhibit about Lupe, including a full replica of her skeleton.

A galvanized steel sculpture of Lupe, a 12,500-year-old Columbian mammoth, along the Guadalupe River Trail near where her fossil was discovered.

life-size galvanized steel replica of Lupe measuring 12 1/2 feet tall and weighing in at nine and a half tons. They placed the massive mammoth along the Guadalupe River Trail near where the bones were discovered.

To find Lupe yourself on foot or by bicycle, watch for her at street level just north of the Trimble Road Bridge. From the south, exit the trail to your right after you pass under the bridge and loop back toward the street. From the north, before you start down the hill under the bridge, exit the trail to your left and see Lupe in front of you.

A BIG DEAL

What: Life-size statue of a fossilized Columbian mammoth discovered nearby on the bank of the Guadalupe River.

Where: The statue is on the Guadalupe River Trail just north of the Mineta San Jose International Airport, near Trimble Rd.

Cost: Free

Pro Tip: Parking is limited in the area.

ON THE TRAIL

What US National Park site is just outside of the city?

The Arrowhead Trail at Coyote Valley Open Space Preserve is an official interpretive site for the Juan Bautista de Anza National Historic Trail. This 1,200-mile, federally designated route stretches from Nogales, Arizona, to San Francisco Bay, and it marks the path traveled by Spanish officer Juan Bautista de Anza to build the first non-native settlements in Northern California. This momentous journey led to the founding of the Pueblo of San Jose, the Presidio of San Francisco, and Catholic missions in San Francisco, Santa Clara, and Fremont.

Over the course of eight months from the fall of 1775 to the spring of 1776, Anza led more than 240 settlers and 100 head of cattle across the deserts on foot and on horseback. The group was said to be one mile wide and three miles long. Each night they set up camp and the next morning packed it all in to head out on the path all over again.

After arriving in the existing military presidio at Monterey, most of the settlers camped there while Anza and a small group of officers and priests carried on toward San Francisco to identify places for a new military encampment, new missions, and residential settlements. On March 24, 1776, this group hiked into the Coyote Valley and set up camp on the banks of

There's a stone monument marking the site where the Anza party camped. It is nine miles south of the preserve along Llagas Creek, adjacent to the Woodland Estates Mobile Home Park and Santa Teresa Boulevard. Park near the clubhouse and then hike west along the creek until you reach the monument at the trail's end.

Looking down over the Coyote Valley from the Arrowhead Trail, Coyote Valley Open Space Preserve.

Llagas Creek in what is now the city of Morgan Hill.

As no land from Anza's actual path is now publicly owned, in 2015 the US National Park Service certified nearby Coyote Valley Open Space Preserve as an interpretive site for the Juan Bautista de Anza National Historic Trail. Visitors hiking the preserve's 4.1-mile Arrowhead Trail can see signage telling the story of this journey, protected landscapes full of native plants and wildlife, and broad views of the valley that Anza and his team traveled through.

SETTLING DOWN

What: The Arrowhead trail at Coyote Valley Open Space Preserve is an official interpretive site of the Juan Bautista de Anza National Historic Trail.

Where: Coyote Valley Open Space Preserve, 550 Palm Ave., Morgan Hill

Cost: Free

Pro Tip: The Santa Clara Valley Open Space Authority hosts regular, free guided hikes to share the story of the Anza expedition.

A THOUSAND DRINKS

How did San Jose become California's first capital?

San Jose was the first civil (nonmilitary, secular) community founded in California, and thanks to lobbying by San Jose–based delegates to the 1849 California Constitutional Convention, the city served as California's first state capital.

The first California legislature met in a hotel in the 100 block of South Market Street that was donated for use by delegate Pierre Sainsevain, a French settler, and the first producer of sparkling wine in California.

This first legislative session was held during a miserable and rainy year. That winter, 36 inches of rain fell on the city, leaving a muddy mess along the road between downtown San Jose and the port at Alviso, the main access point at the time for San Francisco and points north. The roads were so bad that on the opening day of the legislative session only six state senators were able to make it into the new capital city.

The Gold Rush–era state senators were known to be a drunken and carousing lot. At the end of each legislative session (and sometimes midday), Senator Thomas Jefferson Green, never one for moderation, would invite his colleagues to join him by saying, "Well, boys, let's go and take a thousand drinks," or "Let's have a drink! Let's have a thousand drinks!" Though the legislators at that first session did surprisingly get some work done, they became known forever as "The Legislature of a Thousand Drinks."

After one boozy session in San Jose, the state legislature argued about the best location for the state capital. Over the next few years it moved around to various cities, including Vallejo, Benicia, and then finally Sacramento.

The Circle of Palms marks the site where California's first state legislature once met.

"Let's have a drink! Let's have a thousand drinks!" immortalized alongside the Great Seal of California, on the Circle of Palms in downtown San Jose.

Today, San Jose's stunning Circle of Palms Plaza marks the location of that first convening with a ring of tall palm trees. In the center of the circle, look down at the pavement to see the state seal and several historic quotes, including Senator Green's famous call.

FIRST LEGISLATURE

What: Circle of Palms Plaza

Where: 127 S. Market St.

Cost: Free

Pro Tip: To see the spot where the Pueblo of San Jose was first founded, head 2 miles north to the County Civic Center. There's a historic marker near 151 W. Mission St.

TOWERING TOMB

Why isn't there a giant Egyptian pyramid in the middle of San Francisco?

Today, the Bay Area's ego-driven billionaires usually just want to have hospitals named after them. But James Lick, the Gold Rush–era real estate tycoon and once the wealthiest man in California, thought bigger. Much bigger! As his final resting place, he yearned to build the world's largest pyramid—larger than the Great Pyramid of Giza—flanked by 50-foot-tall sculptures of each of his family members, planted at 4th and Market Streets in San Francisco on a block he owned.

Lick made his living as a piano maker in South America, first in Argentina, then Chile and Peru. He came to San Francisco in 1848 with a chest full of $30,000 in gold that he used to buy up vast swaths of soon-to-be valuable land in and around San Francisco, including farmland in San Jose where he built a home and the largest flour mill in the state. He also convinced his friend in Peru, a chocolate maker named Domingo Ghirardelli, that there just might be a market for him in San Francisco.

Luckily for all of us, the eccentric Lick had also befriended many in the San Francisco science community, and these friends turned him away from his pyramid dream and instead encouraged him to build the world's largest telescope at the summit of Mount Hamilton, 25 miles

SHINING STARS

What: Lick Observatory

Where: 7281 Mt. Hamilton Rd., Mt. Hamilton

Cost: Free

Pro Tip: This is an active research facility, and the building is only open to visitors during limited hours, Thursday through Sundays. They offer free talks inside the dome of the 36-inch Great Refractor daily. See the website for the schedule. If you want to look through the giant telescope, get a ticket for one of the Summer Series evening events. They sell out fast!

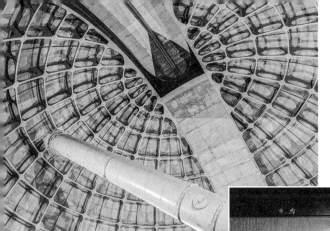

Lick Observatory's Great Lick Refractor was the largest refracting telescope in the world for more than a decade after the research facility was built.

James Lick's final resting place beneath the telescope.

east of San Jose. In 1874, Lick bequeathed the largest portion of his estate, $700,000, or more than $17 million in today's dollars, to the University of California to build an observatory and refractor on this high peak. To mark his legacy, Lick asked that his body be buried on the site just beneath the giant telescope.

A year later, James Lick Observatory was completed, and the 36-inch Great Lick Refractor was the largest refracting telescope in the world for almost a decade. Researchers used the telescope to discover the fifth moon of Jupiter, the first such discovery since Galileo discovered the first four almost three centuries earlier.

Today, UC faculty and students operate state-of-the-art equipment at the site. The observatory is rarely open to the public at night because the telescopes are in use almost every night of the year.

You can see James Lick's mansion and old granary hidden inside the aptly named Mansion Grove Apartments (502 Mansion Park Dr.) in Santa Clara.

SECRETS IN THE STACKS

What strange features lie hidden in the MLK Library?

At first glance, the Dr. Martin Luther King, Jr. Library seems like any other big city library. But if you look a little closer, you'll find dozens of strange things, such as mirrors hidden behind stacks of books, rows that greet you with the mysterious sound of pages turning, and even a secret trap door.

These treasures are just a few pieces in a collection of conceptual art called "Recolleciones," created by artist Mel Chin. This project discreetly integrates 34 different weird and wonderful works of art into the library, adjacent to book collections that are relevant to the theme.

As an example, the aforementioned hidden mirrors are a work called "Self-Help Mirrors," and you'll find them buried in the stacks near the psychology and self-help collection, imploring us to look inward and reflect on ourselves to find the solutions to our problems. The work "Page Passage" is an audio installation where you hear the sound of pages turning when you go down the aisle, and "Fiction/Fiction" is a secret rotating bookcase with faux-mystery books on one side and current popular titles on the other. Can you tell the real fiction from the fake fiction?

The Dr. Martin Luther King, Jr. Library is jointly owned by the City of San Jose and San Jose Public Library system. When it opened in 2003, it was the only joint city/university library in the United States, and it has since inspired a few other similar urban partnerships.

"Skeptacle," shares the productive work of generations of "busy bees," displaying San Jose State student theses.

HIDDEN TREASURES

What: Dr. Martin Luther King, Jr. Library

Where: 150 E. San Fernando St.

Cost: Free

Pro Tip: Free guided drop-in tours are given every Thursday at 11:30 a.m.

Other works are inspired by the history of the Santa Clara Valley. In "Round Up," 81 yellow leather desk chairs are marked with the cattle brand of the original San Jose rancho families circa 1819. The chairs are hidden in plain sight at tables throughout the library. Mounted near the labor history section is "Gong and Scale," a giant model of a Chinese gong alongside the San Jose Scale (*Quadraspidiotus perniciosus*), an invasive insect that destroyed grapevines and orchards in the 1880s. Chinese laborers were wrongly blamed for bringing this infestation, and the racial dissent spurred one of San Jose's first labor strikes.

While you can explore these works of art on your own using the guide on the library's website, they offer free guided tours every Thursday morning or by appointment, depending on docent availability.

TICKLED IVORIES

Where can you enjoy a chorus of self-playing pianos?

Orchestria Palm Court is half restaurant and half vintage technology museum, letting you take a trip back in time and dine as you might have a hundred years ago.

Owner Mark Williams started the restaurant in a historic 1910 auto showroom in the South First Arts District as a way to share his personal collection of mechanical instruments. These include almost a dozen self-playing pianos, early jukeboxes, a phonograph, a self-playing violin, and two "orchestrions," instruments that replicate the sound of an entire orchestra by merging the sounds of several instruments using the same music roll. These low-tech mechanical instruments were popular in bars and restaurants in the early 20th century. The project is a labor of love and only open Friday and Saturday nights. Williams works full-time during the week as an electrical engineer.

As you dine, the instruments that line the walls of the dining room are programmed to play, one by one, hopping back and forth across the restaurant. You never know when the piano right next to you will turn on and start to belt out a tune.

IN TUNE

What: Orchestria Palm Court

Where: 27 E. William St.

Cost: Food and drink prices vary; the tunes are free!

Pro Tip: No tipping; a service fee is included in the price of your meal. They are only open Friday and Saturday nights and fill up fast, so reservations are strongly recommended.

An old-fashioned working phone booth invites guests to test it out by calling their dining companions or friends.

One of the many player pianos at Orchestria Palm Court belts out a tune.

Take a "sip" back in time with one of the restaurant's old-fashioned fountain sodas.

Bookcases line the wall stacked top to bottom with old piano rolls, and period decor, including Tiffany lamps and Art Deco stained glass period decor.

Try the handcrafted sodas, popular during the Prohibition Era. The restaurant's "soda jerk" handcrafts a dozen vintage recipe alcohol-free drinks, such as Poppy Dew, Raspberry Ambrosia, and Black Forest and Chocolate Phosphates.

ENLIGHTENING EATS

Where can you find heavenly vegan food?

San Jose has the largest number of Vietnamese residents of any city outside of Vietnam, and not surprisingly, many wonderful Vietnamese restaurants. But the most interesting way to experience Vietnamese food isn't in one of those restaurants. It's at a Buddhist temple.

Duc Vien Buddhist Community Pagoda (Chùa Đức Viên) was founded by a nun named Đàm Lựu back in 1980, and the verdant grounds and ornate temple offer a peaceful respite from the city, just steps away from the congestion of Tully Road. Uniquely, it's the only Buddhist temple run entirely by women in Northern California. The complex is home to about 50 nuns who have dedicated their lives to the practice of Pure Land Buddhism. Each Sunday the temple is packed with families coming for worship and children's Vietnamese language classes.

Every Sunday, temple volunteers set up tents in the rear courtyard and sell a variety of sweet and savory Vietnamese dishes, all made vegetarian according to Buddhist principles. On a recent weekend, these included popular Vietnamese soups, such as bún riêu, a fresh tomato and tofu noodle soup; and bún bò Huế, a spicy faux beef (vegetarian) noodle soup. The food is offered for free to the nuns and visiting monks, but guests are asked to donate for the meals, and all proceeds go to support the nuns and their community service. Guests are expected to wash their own trays and dishes at an outdoor wash station using a series of water bins to rinse them clean.

Don't miss visiting the temple during the Lunar New Year when they have food stalls open through the first week of the year.

14

Some of the sweet and savory treats for sale on a typical Sunday.

FOODIE FUNDRAISING

What: Street food stalls every Sunday at Duc Vien Buddhist Community Pagoda

Where: 2440 McLaughlin Ave.

Cost: Suggested donation varies.

Pro Tip: Bring cash. Parking in the on-site lot is limited, so be prepared to park in a neighborhood and walk over. This is an active place of worship, so be sure to dress modestly and take off your shoes before entering.

Visit at the Lunar New Year when the temple is decorated with colorful flowers and lanterns, and visitors pack the grounds morning to night to light incense and pray for a prosperous new year. Additionally, volunteers sell traditional New Year's foods, such as bánh chứng, rice cake wrapped in bamboo leaf, and popular sweet treats, such as bright green pandan and coconut waffles, and different types of chè, a sweet rice pudding.

OF UNKNOWN ORIGIN

Who built these mysterious stone walls?

In the hills north of San Jose, there's a portion of an old rock wall that's deeply shrouded in mystery. This structure is one of several segments stretching from Ed R. Levin County Park in Milpitas all the way up to the Berkeley Hills. There are no records of who built them, how old they are, why they were built, and they don't even appear on historic property maps. They've been nicknamed the East Bay "Mystery Walls."

The first time the word "mystery" was used in relation to these walls was in an 1896 article in the *San Francisco Chronicle*. "Half a mile east of Grizzly Peak stand the remnants of stone walls which have long baffled the researches and curiosity of antiquarians," the author said. "By whom they were erected, when and why is an unsolved mystery."

While researchers, including Jeff Fentress, an archaeologist from San Francisco State University, can't comment with certainty on the origin of these walls, they suspect these are magical explanations for a very normal and everyday thing.

"A few years before the Gold Rush, there were only a few hundred non-Indian people in San Francisco," Fentress said. "Two years after the Gold Rush, there were 200,000 people here. A lot of these people were running sheep and cattle, and they had to keep their herds separate from everyone else."

A 1995 survey by the East Bay Regional Park district presented a comprehensive review of literature on the walls

---

Locals have speculated that these walls were built by Vikings, the Vatican, Aztec warriors, Chinese explorers, and even people from the mythical lost land of Lemuria.

You can spot the walls, and get a great view of the Bay, by hiking the Monument Peak Trail at Ed R. Levin County Park.

including one other prominent theory, that "the Franciscans of Mission San Jose directed the construction of the walls using their native converts as labor." Documents from the Mission reveal that the native people raised cattle as part of the Spanish system of forced labor.

Whether magical or mundane, the walls remain a source of curiosity for visitors from around the Bay.

WALK THE WALLS

What: The southernmost segment of the walls at Ed R. Levin County Park.

Where: 3100 Calaveras Rd., Milpitas

Cost: $6 vehicle admission fee.

Pro Tip: Start at Sandy Wool Lake and take the Tularcitos Trail to the Agua Caliente Trail and then up to the Monument Peak Trail. Follow the Monument Peak Trail all the way to the peak. This challenging hike (3 miles one way with 1,250 feet of elevation gain) will take about three hours.

A MOO WITH A VIEW

Why are there so many cows on local hiking trails?

If you've ever gone hiking in the hills around the South Bay, you've probably noticed the cows—fields of cattle grazing public lands in view of the city even in areas crossed by hiking trails. It might seem an unusual sight to see cattle ranching so close to downtown San Jose.

While the Santa Clara Valley has had a ranching industry since Spanish colonists brought livestock to the region in the 1700s, there's more to the continued cattle ranching than the desire to protect that heritage, though that is one reason why our local governments support protecting small ranches and farms.

In fact, those cows are working hard to help protect our environment. Public land management agencies including Santa Clara County Parks & Recreation, Santa Clara Valley Open Space Authority, and Midpeninsula Open Space District are taking advantage of the bovine preference for fast-growing (and apparently tasty) invasive grasses and shrubs. Grazing cattle have been shown to offer many

LIVESTOCK LAND STEWARDS

What: Protected open spaces in the hills and valleys around San Jose.

Where: Sierra Vista Open Space Preserve, Joseph D. Grant County Park, and other local parks.

Cost: Free

Pro Tip: Watch out for cow patties on the trail! And be sure to close the cattle gates behind you.

Agriculture is not just part of our past. In 2018, Santa Clara County had more than 1,000 farms with a total economic production value of $1.6 billion.

Cattle grazing in the hills and protected open spaces in and around San Jose. Photo courtesy of the Santa Clara Valley Open Space Authority

You might be sharing the trail with a herd of cows on this hike at Sierra Vista Open Space Preserve.

benefits to California grasslands. Cattle reduce the growth and density of invasive plant species, protect native plant and animal diversity, and help prevent catastrophic wildfires by reducing highly flammable dry grasses. By allowing controlled grazing according to plans developed by an ecologist, the agencies are working to protect native species and protect our communities from wildfires.

So, the next time you see cows out on a hike, thank them for their service!

REST IN PIECES

Where can you honor the memory of an amputated arm?

The most famous grave in the village of New Almaden's cemetery is not that of a whole human body. In 1893, a 13-year-old boy named Richard Bertram ("Bert") Barrett shot off his arm in a hunting accident in the Almaden Hills. He survived, but in accordance with local law of the time, his family buried the severed limb at nearby Hacienda Cemetery. Still today you can go to this tiny cemetery to see the fading wooden gravestone marked, "His arm lies here. May it rest in peace." Local legend says that each year on Halloween Night, Barrett's arm comes alive, rises out of the tomb, and tries to reunite with the rest of Bert's body that was buried 61 years later and 11 miles away at San Jose's Oak Hill Memorial Park.

The village of New Almaden was the gateway to the New Almaden Quicksilver Mine, once the largest mercury mine in the United States. For many years, miners used mercury to

A LOST LIMB

What: Hacienda Cemetery

Where: 21440 Bertram Rd.

Cost: Free

Pro Tip: The grave is located in the southern part of the cemetery, which is bisected by Bertram Rd., named for Bert's family. You can park along the side of the road.

Be sure to visit the New Almaden Quicksilver Mining Museum (21350 Almaden Rd.) to learn about the community's mining history and explore the hidden village of New Almaden. Pick up a town map with a self-guided walking tour from the museum's gift store.

Bert Barrett's (arm's) grave at Hacienda Cemetery in the village of New Almaden.

Exhibits at the New Almaden Quicksilver Mining Museum share stories of the workers who mined these hills.

extract gold from rock, so the New Almaden Mine helped make the Gold Rush possible. At peak, the hills were home to more than 4,000 miners and their families. Today, the mines are closed, and the site is a ghost town protected as a Santa Clara County park. You can visit the park and hike the trails to explore the relics of the old company town.

CRISIS AVERTED

Was San Jose close to joining the Confederacy?

In 1863, in the middle of the Civil War, President Lincoln got himself ensnared in a land rights case that came surprisingly close to sparking a battle for secession right here in San Jose.

The New Almaden Quicksilver Mining Company had been founded in 1845 by a Mexican lieutenant and sold in 1850 to a Mexican mine operator. After California joined the Union the same year, the US government, swayed by East Coast mining interests, particularly the Quicksilver Mining Company of New York that owned mines near New Almaden, argued that the land claim was based on fraudulent documents and the land should revert to the US government. Curiously, several Lincoln administration officials held stock in the Quicksilver Mining Company. This claim was even upheld by the US Supreme Court.

On May 8, 1863, President Lincoln authorized an agent to go to New Almaden and take possession of the land for the United States. US military forces were engaged in case they would have to take the land by force.

On July 9, Lincoln's agent traveled to the New Almaden mine and demanded that the mine manager turn the land over to the US government. The mine manager refused. Word of this attempt to take control of the mine spread through communities of miners in both California and Nevada who feared this would lead to other takeovers and that they would

---

Though California was technically a free state, some Southerners brought their slaves with them to work on farms or in mines. In the 1852 census, the occupation of "slave" was listed for eight people in Santa Clara County.

A Civil War history exhibit at the New Almaden Quicksilver Mining Museum.

lose their jobs. Newspapers showed cartoons of miners in mass revolt holding signs saying, "Lincoln, you won't take our mines! Stay out of New Almaden!"

While California was officially part of the Union, 10 percent of the population was thought to support Confederate causes, including slavery. Southern political sympathizers exploited the miners' fear of the US government.

Lincoln's officials in San Francisco warned the president that an armed uprising at New Almaden was likely and could have broader political implications of spreading Confederate support across the West if he moved forward with plans to take the mines.

Lincoln took the advice of his colleagues on the ground in California and decided to back off and issued an apology, leaving companies to resolve these issues on their own. Ultimately, the New Almaden Company wound up selling the property to the Quicksilver Mining Company anyway. Lincoln maintained the support he needed and won the votes of a majority of California voters in his reelection the following year.

MINE STORIES

What: New Almaden Quicksilver Mining Museum

Where: 21350 Almaden Rd.

Cost: Free

Pro Tip: To learn more about the Almaden Mines and the workers who toiled below ground, check out the county park's website and join one of the free historic hikes that docents lead each month.

MONUMENT TO NOWHERE

What political stunt by a city council member got a freeway segment named after him?

When you cross the massive four-level freeway interchange at the junction of highways 101, 280, and 680 you may not know that this piece of infrastructure was named for an epic publicity stunt.

In the mid-1970s, construction of the interchange was stalled for several years by the state due to reported lack of funding. This left an unfinished, 100-foot-long highway overpass segment suspended in the air and thousands of frustrated local motorists.

In 1976, San Jose city councilman Joe Colla wanted to call attention to this broken promise and alleged diversion of state highway funding. Colla and colleagues, including a local building trades union official, paid a crane operator to lift a 1960 Chevy Impala up onto the overpass in the dark of the night. First thing the next morning,

UP ON HIGH

What: The Joe Colla Interchange

Where: The interchange connecting Interstate 280, Interstate 680, and US Route 101.

Cost: Free

Pro Tip: Watch for "Joe Colla Interchange" marker signs along each of these stretches of freeway.

The concrete "highway in the sky" sat half-finished, suspended 200 feet above ground for almost five years before Colla's prank.

This photo of San Jose City councilmember Joe Colla's 1976 stunt went viral and got state legislators to fund the eventual completion of this long-delayed highway overpass. Photo courtesy of History San Jose

Colla hopped aboard a private helicopter that took off from San Jose State's Spartan Stadium and transported him to the top of the unfinished interchange. The photos of Colla and a lone car perched atop the lonely interchange spread around the state and got then California Governor Jerry Brown to call the head of the Operating Engineers union to demand they take the car down right away.

The resulting media attention and additional on-the-ground organizing work by the now famous Colla finally influenced the state legislature to approve funding, and builders went back to work, completing the interchange five years later.

In 2010, the state legislature approved a resolution naming the interchange after this local activist.

SÍ, SE PUEDE

What American civil rights icon got started organizing in San Jose?

The legendary civil rights leader César Chávez is usually associated with his work organizing for farmworker rights in California's Central Valley. But almost a decade before he moved to rural Kern County to help found what would become the United Farm Workers (UFW), he found his calling as an activist fighting for the rights of local people here in San Jose.

Chávez was born in Yuma, Arizona, to Mexican-American farmworker parents who moved his family to California when he was young, eventually settling in East San Jose. Their immigrant community had poor housing and infrastructure, including rutted dirt roads that flooded every time it rained. Locals called the neighborhood "Sal Si Puedes," or "Get Out If You Can."

Chávez was active in the eastside Catholic church, Our Lady of Guadalupe Mission Chapel. In 1952, Father Donald McDonnell got to know Chávez and identified him as a potential leader who could help organize his neighbors to push for changes in their neighborhood, and he introduced him to the growing Latino civil rights organization, the Community Service Organization (CSO).

For the next decade, Chávez worked with the CSO honing his skills in organizing first local and then state and national politics by canvassing door-to-door, planning community meetings, and registering people to vote. Inspired by the poor working conditions farmworkers faced in the Santa Clara Valley and

The house where César and his wife, Helen Chávez, lived (53 Scharff Ave.) is marked by a historic plaque. It's a private residence, so do not disturb the residents.

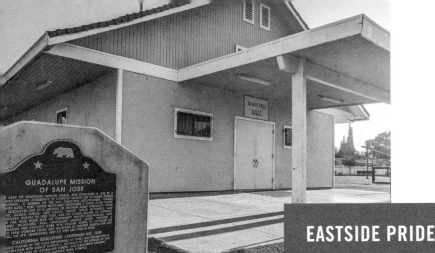

The meeting hall at Our Lady of Guadalupe Parish, where civil rights leader César Chávez got his start organizing his East San Jose neighbors in the fight to improve their community.

EASTSIDE PRIDE

What: Our Lady of Guadalupe Parish

Where: 2020 E. San Antonio St.

Cost: Free

Pro Tip: You can view McDonnell Hall where Chávez and other community activists held their first meetings and a mosaic on the side of the chapel that honors Chávez's legacy. This is an active community of worship, so don't disturb the parishioners.

beyond, he moved to the Central Valley in 1962 to help build a national farmworker movement, winning the first ever farmworker union contract, and state and national legislation to help improve the lives of agricultural and immigrant workers.

Our Lady of Guadalupe Parish continues to serve the eastside community and provide a place of respite. The church and neighboring McDonnell Hall, where Chávez and other community activists held their first meetings, has been named both a state and a National Historic Landmark for this important legacy. Some of Chávez's family members still live in San Jose and run a local foundation that honors César's memory by giving scholarships to Northern California youth.

THE PEOPLE'S THEATER

What storytelling tradition grew out of San Jose?

Luis Valdez is the writer and director of *Zoot Suit* and *La Bamba* and is considered to be the father of Chicano theater in the United States. He got his start in theater as a student at San Jose State, where he wrote and produced his first full-length play in 1964.

After college, Valdez was drawn to the Central Valley during the Delano Grape Strike led by labor activists César Chávez and Dolores Huerta. He envisioned a theater company that would be of, by, and for farmworkers and that would be a source of expression, protest, and entertainment. This project became known as "El Teatro Campesino" (Farmworker's Theater), where striking workers act out short sketches about the need for a union right on the picket lines.

COMMUNITY THEATER

What: Teatro Visión

Where: School of Arts & Culture at Mexican Heritage Plaza, 1700 Alum Rock Ave.

Cost: Varies

Pro Tip: Tickets are priced on a sliding scale, based on how much you can pay. All productions are bilingual, English and Spanish, and many include American Sign Language interpretation.

Valdez credits his time at San Jose State for inspiring him to be both an artist and an activist. "I was really looking and trying to find a path for myself, not just as a playwright but as an activist," he says. "Really, my involvement in the cultural revolution started on the campus."

From a 2019 performance of "Macario," by Teatro Visión. Photo courtesy of Nicole Pérez, Cherry Pink Productions

Valdez described his theater as a way to give a voice to the voiceless, reflect on the world, and share what it is to be a Chicano in the United States. The theater recognizes injustices people have faced, shares their stories with humanity and dignity, and empowers them to resist.

While you can visit Valdez's El Teatro Campesino, now based as a permanent theater company in San Juan Bautista, San Jose's Teatro Visión shares this purpose closer to home. This local theater arts company inspires Chicanx and Latinx writers and performers to share their stories and challenge the traditional narratives that have been imposed on them and their communities.

MOUNTAIN CHARLIE

What local pioneer lost part of his skull in a grizzly bear attack and lived to tell the tale?

Back before our forefathers drove the species extinct in the state, thousands of California grizzly bears roamed the valleys and mountains of Northern California. Known for their size, strength, and beauty, these bears were the symbol of the California Republic, an independent breakaway nation movement that controlled an area north of San Francisco for 25 days in 1846. Later, the bear was included on California's official state flag and became our official state animal.

The last grizzly ever spotted in the Santa Cruz Mountains was killed in 1885 near the town of Bonny Doon. One reason for the decline, no doubt, was the gruesome bear versus bull fights that were popular entertainment in 19th century California. Every Sunday afternoon, spectators could come to San Jose's St. James Square to place bets as these giants were pitted against each other to the death.

One of San Jose's most famous bear fights, though, involved Charles "Mountain Charlie" (sometimes spelled "Charley") McKiernan, one of the first settlers in the Santa Cruz Mountains. McKiernan was a skilled hunter and outdoorsman and sold fresh venison and sometimes bear meat at markets in San Francisco.

In one not-so-lucky hunting trip in 1854, McKiernan came face-to-face with a grizzly mother and her cubs. The bear whacked him to the ground and tore out a portion of his skull. McKiernan's friend carried him on horseback into San Jose

---

Mountain Charlie is buried in San Jose's Oak Hill Memorial Park in the northwest corner of Section Q, Block 121.

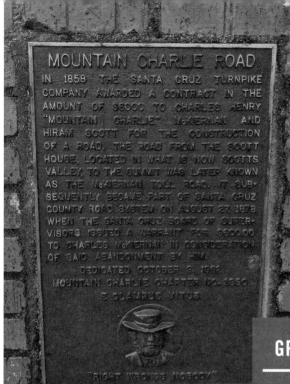

MOUNTAIN CHARLIE ROAD

IN 1858 THE SANTA CRUZ TURNPIKE
COMPANY AWARDED A CONTRACT IN THE
AMOUNT OF $6000 TO CHARLES HENRY
"MOUNTAIN CHARLIE" McKIERNAN AND
HIRAM SCOTT FOR THE CONSTRUCTION
OF A ROAD. THE ROAD FROM THE SCOTT
HOUSE, LOCATED IN WHAT IS NOW SCOTTS
VALLEY, TO THE SUMMIT WAS LATER KNOWN
AS THE McKIERNAN TOLL ROAD. IT SUB-
SEQUENTLY BECAME PART OF SANTA CRUZ
COUNTY ROAD SYSTEM ON AUGUST 27, 1878
WHEN THE SANTA CRUZ BOARD OF SUPER-
VISORS ISSUED A WARRANT FOR $600.00
TO CHARLES McKIERNAN IN CONSIDERATION
OF SAID ABANDONMENT BY HIM

DEDICATED OCTOBER 3, 1982
MOUNTAIN CHARLIE CHAPTER NO. 1850
E CLAMPUS VITUS

"RIGHT WRONGS NOBODY"

Historic marker on "Mountain Charlie Road," the first toll road over the hill from Los Gatos to Santa Cruz.

GRIN & BEAR IT

What: The first road connecting the Santa Clara Valley through Los Gatos to Santa Cruz, built by Charlie McKiernan.

Where: Mountain Charlie Rd.

Cost: Free

Pro Tip: Find a memorial plaque at the northernmost end of Mountain Charlie Rd. near the Summit Road Overpass. Pick and cut your own Christmas tree at the seasonal Mountain Charlie Ranch tree farm.

where he could see a doctor. McKiernan survived thanks to the doctors who installed a metal plate in his head, without the use of anesthetics that were not yet available. Two years later, he needed the surgery redone to treat an infection. Luckily by that time, his doctor was able to use the new anesthetic, chloroform, the first time it was used in the region. Mountain Charlie was self-conscious of his scars and was never spotted without a brimmed hat pulled far down over his eyebrows.

HOLY ROLLERS

When did a racist cult run a popular highway rest stop?

The Santa Cruz Mountains have always attracted eccentric people drawn to the remote landscape. The 19th century stagecoach and railroad route between San Jose and Santa Cruz are now ghost towns—Alma, Patchen, and Laurel to name a few. By far the most unusual of these pre-Highway 17 communities was Holy City. This tourist trap and summit rest stop was founded in 1918 by "Father" William E. Riker, where he lived with about 30 of his followers.

Followers of Riker's self-styled religion, "The Perfect Christian Divine Way," made vows of celibacy and abstinence from alcohol. Of course, Riker himself, who had several wives and fled the state at one point to escape bigamy charges, was apparently exempt from the former. Riker was also a white supremacist who preached total segregation of races and even corresponded with Adolf Hitler during World War II.

To make money and gain converts, the community built a gas station, restaurant, and ice cream parlor plastered with extravagant signs sharing Riker's ramblings and racist beliefs. Despite these unholy proclamations, the local post office was allegedly busy during the holiday season as many San Jose families made the trip up the hill to get their Christmas cards stamped with the Holy City postmark.

The community declined after 1940 when Highway 17 opened, diverting people away from the old Santa Cruz Highway. A series of mysterious fires burned down most

Hawaiian Punch was said to have been invented at the Holy City soda fountain.

Flashy roadside signs lured drivers heading over the hill from San Jose to Santa Cruz to stop in Holy City. Photo courtesy of History San Jose

of the remaining structures in the late 1950s. Riker ran unsuccessfully for governor of California four times, although you're probably wondering how he could lose with campaign signs that promised he was "the only man who can save California from going plum to Hell." Toward the end of his life, Riker was pushed out as leader of the community in 1960. Three years later he converted to Catholicism, and passed away in 1969 at the age of 96.

MOUNTAIN CULT

What: Site of a cult that operated a quirky roadside stand and rest stop on the old road to Santa Cruz.

Where: Near the intersection of Holy City Rd. and the Old Santa Cruz Hwy.

Cost: Cost of gas/EV charge to get into the hills

Pro Tip: While the last remaining business that carried the town's name, Holy City Art Glass, closed in 2015, the shop's founder, artist Tom Stanton's legacy lives on in the Magical Glass Pumpkin Patch, an annual hand-blown art glass pumpkin sale fundraiser for Los Gatos High School.

PEDAL TO POULTRY

How can you take a tour of backyard chicken coops?

One weekend each spring, South Bay families have a "clucking good time" opening up their homes for a unique tour.

BACKYARD INSPIRATION

What: The annual Silicon Valley Tour de Coop, a self-guided bike tour of local chicken coops, beehives, and sustainable homesteads who open their homes to the public for one day each spring.

Where: Self-guided tour. RSVP on the event's website (https://tourdecoop.org) and the organizers will send you a list of participating homes.

Cost: Free

Pro Tip: Attendees are invited to get their "Tour de Coop Chicken Hat," a printable chicken image downloadable from the event's website to print and attach to your bike helmet.

The Tour de Coop is a self-guided bike tour of backyard chicken coops, beehives, and backyard farms from San Jose to Palo Alto.

This volunteer-led annual event started seven years ago when the founder, Scott Vanderlip, heard about a small chicken coop tour in Davis, California. He worked with some friends to organize a similar event here in Silicon Valley to give the community inspiration for sustainable living. With Silicon Valley's high density of environmentally conscious folks and creative tinkerers, the event took off. As Vanderlip said, "Chickens cross every demographic, economic boundary, gender, and race."

In 2018, more than 32 families (called "coopsters") agreed to open up their backyards as stops, and 2,500 participants registered to join the tour.

As the event has grown, organizers have been able to map the participating homes into several citywide loop tours,

34

Thinking of getting backyard chickens? Ask questions and get inspiration from the neighbors who open up their homes on this tour.

Participants on the Tour de Coop, a self-guided bike tour of local chicken coops and backyard farms. Photos courtesy of Scott Vanderlip.

so even families with small kids can bike to the homes in their neighborhood. Participants take pictures of the projects and get inspiration for their own coops and urban homestead projects.

Tour de Coop draws both liberal environmentalists seeking to reduce their carbon footprint and libertarian "preppers" interested in self-reliant food production.

EGG-CELLENT

What are "checks and dirties"?

You probably know a few things about eggs—there are conventional, organic, sometimes free range, and you can usually buy them in one of two colors, white or brown.

But one little corner store on Sierra Road offers many more options. Olivera Egg Ranch is a family-owned egg farm that has had a farm store in the east hills for decades. Though their poultry farm is in Tracy, they sell a wide variety of eggs at the San Jose store. For chicken eggs, they have regular and organic, white and brown, but also other options: small, large, and extra large; Grade AA (the freshest, unlike the Grade A commonly found in stores); crates of 12 or 18, and flats of 30; double yolk; and duck, goose, and quail eggs.

They also have another budget-friendly option you won't see anywhere else: "Checks and Dirties"—slightly irregular eggs with either fractured shells that don't perforate the membrane or eggs with some visible dirt or a stained shell. While California law doesn't allow restaurants or bakeries to make and sell products made with these visually imperfect eggs, they are okay to eat, though the store does recommend you try to consume them quickly. Beyond the eggs, the store also sells fresh and frozen chicken, basic grocery items, and some unique treats like homemade Portuguese sweet bread.

THIS IS CUCKOO

What: Olivera Egg Ranch

Where: 3315 Sierra Rd.

Cost: Prices vary

Pro Tip: No photos allowed.

Find eggs of every variety at Olivera Egg Ranch.

"Fresher! Tastier!"

If you're feeling adventurous, ask for balut at the register. It's a fertilized egg that contains a partially developed embryo and is considered a delicacy in the Philippines.

MANE ATTRACTION

Where can you see Beethoven's hair?

Ludwig van Beethoven's wild and unruly hair is an iconic part of the legendary German composer's image as a tortured artist and you can see it here in San Jose!

The Ira F. Brilliant Center for Beethoven Studies at San Jose State University owns one of the world's largest collections of Beethoven's first edition music, historic instruments, rare books, artwork, and other documents related to his work. The research center also owns several locks of the composer's hair, clipped when he was on his deathbed. Back in the days before photography was invented, this was one of the ways people remembered and honored the dead.

One of the bodily relics in the collection is known as the Guevara Lock, a collection of 3- to 6-inch salt-and-pepper colored hairs. Using samples taken from this lock 150 years after the composer's death, scientists were able to identify lead poisoning as the likely cause of the 56-year-old composer's death and many

SNIPS IN THE STACKS

What: Ira F. Brilliant Center for Beethoven Studies

Where: Dr. Martin Luther King, Jr. Library, 150 E. San Fernando St.

Cost: Free

Pro Tip: The Beethoven Center is located in Room 580 in the special collections area on the fifth floor of the library.

The book *The Mysteries of Beethoven's Hair* by Russell Martin shares the story of the Guevara Lock and how it made its way around Europe during World War II.

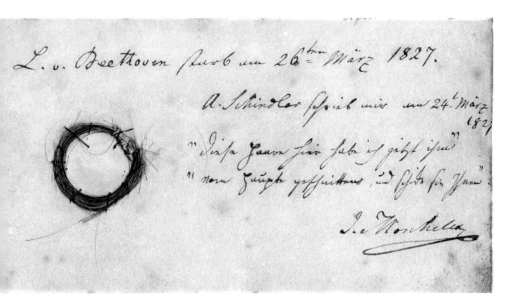

The collection owns several locks of Ludwig von Beethoven's hair, cut on his deathbed in 1827. Photo from the collections of the Ira F. Brilliant Center for Beethoven Studies, San Jose State University

ailments that plagued him near the end of his life. While the Guevara Lock is no longer on display because of continued research, the collection does have two other locks of his hair on display as well as a reproduction of the "death mask," a plaster impression of Beethoven's face captured after he died.

FURRY FRIENDS

What annual conference encourages people to dress as their "fursona"?

When you are driving through downtown and see a pack of 6-foot-tall dogs and cats crossing the street, you know it's probably Further Confusion (FurCon), an international gathering of more than four thousand animal-loving costumers held each January in San Jose.

Members of the "furry fandom," or "furries" as they are called, branched out of the broader comic and anime world in the 1990s. Attendees, whether in costume or not, often hold a "fursona"—a virtual character-driven animal identity that they take and use in the online world and at these conventions. Some attendees have more than one fursona, and even full head-to-toe costumes called "fursuits" that they wear on different days, as the mood strikes.

Not all convention goers wear a head-to-toe fursuit, though most attendees I asked aspire to have one someday. These custom-designed costumes can cost several thousand dollars, so they are not accessible to everyone. Some attendees just wear a big fluffy tail or paws

---

PAW PATROL

What: Further Confusion

Where: San Jose McEnery Convention Center, 150 W. San Carlos St.

Cost: Conference admission varies

Pro Tip: If you hang out anywhere downtown during FurCon weekend, you'll see the furries at local restaurants and bars.

Not all furries have fur. Some attendees come dressed as reptiles, birds, and insects.

Meeting "furries" at Further Confusion, January 2020.

and feet, or the head, as they work on building their costume bit by bit. It's the only place (I hope!) I'll ever overhear someone say, "Here's an Ikea bag full of dog parts."

Attendees say the San Jose convention is one of their favorites. People are more friendly than other furry conventions. Also, the venue is a close walk to downtown bars and restaurants, and welcoming locals never bat an eye when they walk in.

FORGING AHEAD

Where can you learn to make a medieval weapon?

Have you ever dreamed of pounding hot steel, heated over a roaring furnace, but gave up because you thought this art was lost to history? San Jose's School of Visual Philosophy is a nonprofit arts education organization that offers a variety of workshops in creative disciplines, from common ideas of visual art, such as figure sculpting and painting, to older and formerly vocational arts, such as bronze casting, blacksmithing, and screen printing.

On a recent visit to the school, I observed a small group of about 10 students learning the basics of ironworking by making a Baltic javelin, a curved blade that would be mounted on a wooden spear and used in both hunting and war from the 11th to the 13th centuries.

It was beautiful to watch school co-founder and instructor, Yori Seeger, heat up a chunky steel plate over a flame until it glowed red, and then hammer it until it lengthened and thinned into the shape of a blade. The students in the class ranged from a teenager there with his

IRON AGE

What: School of Visual Philosophy

Where: 1065 The Alameda

Cost: Varies

Pro Tip: No synthetic fabrics allowed (your clothing will melt!)

"It was cool to be in a place that doesn't treat a blacksmith like a novelty," said School of Visual Philosophy co-founder Yori Seeger regarding meeting working blacksmiths on a family trip to Tallinn, Estonia.

Seeger demonstrating the proper hammering technique.

The step-by-step transformation of a stick of iron to a blade.

parents to 20-something enthusiasts of medieval role-playing video games and even retirees. Half the students were women.

Besides the educational component, the organization helps support and incubate new artists and creative organizations. They rent out space to more than 30 individual artists and a few small companies. For the long term, they aspire to get accredited and become a certificate-granting art school.

SECONDHAND CHIC

What upscale boutique is hidden within a chain thrift store?

At first glance, the Goodwill of Silicon Valley store on San Carlos Street seems like your typical thrift store. But if you follow the signs and climb the stairs to the second floor, you'll enter a new world with sleek wooden floors and retro decor, such as vintage turntables and historic photos of San Jose. The Loft is a project of the local thrift chain, and features lightly used, second-hand designer and name-brand clothing and accessories from brands like Tory Burch, Lululemon, Patagonia, Ted Baker, Coach, and Cole Haan.

Unlike independent vintage and consignment shops that depend on intentional solicitation by donors or who have a single buyer to source items, Goodwill is able to curate the "best of the best" from items donated to their 18 retail stores in Santa Clara County. Vice President of Retail, Stephen Borasi, estimates that less than 5 percent of all items donated to the chain are considered for this highly curated collection. While prices are higher than a typical Goodwill store, the Loft still offers deep discounts off retail. You might find a designer leather bag that would sell for $250 at Nordstrom on sale for $50 at The Loft.

The organization opened The Loft in 2016 after buying the building next door and merging the two units. Goodwill has not done any paid advertising to promote the unique concept

THRIFTY THREADS

What: The Loft Boutique

Where: Goodwill of Silicon Valley, 1691 W. San Carlos St.

Cost: Varies

Pro Tip: Downstairs is a normal Goodwill store. Follow the signs upstairs to The Loft.

*Find high-end and antique secondhand steals at
The Loft by Goodwill of Silicon Valley.*

store. News of it spread mostly by word of mouth, and it's been very successful, exceeding original sales goals. They've since added an e-commerce division, selling selected items through their website and on eBay. As a bonus, all proceeds benefit the organization's job development and social service programs for military veterans, people with developmental disabilities, and the formerly incarcerated.

On the store's first day of business, they sold an antique platinum diamond ring for $5,000.

COWBOYS AND ICE CREAM

Where can you gear up for the rodeo and get an ice cream cone?

El Nuevo Rancho Grande on Alum Rock in East San Jose is a one-stop shop for all of your tropical ice cream and Western wear needs.

On one side of the store there's an ice cream stand serving a variety of homemade Mexican ice creams (helados), sorbets (nieves), and popsicles (paletas). The sweet treats feature unique, tropical, and regional ingredients, such as guava, prickly pear cactus, mamey sapote, piña colada, and arroz con leche (rice pudding).

On the other side of the store, you'll see rows of wide and pointy-tipped cowboy boots (vaqueros) in every color of the rainbow. Some are made of rare and unusual leathers, such as snake, ostrich, and alligator skin. The store also carries all manner of cowboy hats, embroidered Western and regional clothing (such as Cuban guayaberas), belts, buckles, and more.

While San Jose is no longer the Wild West, this clothing appeals to San Jose's large Northern Mexican community—from such states as Sonora, Chihuahua, Sinaloa, and other rural regions. You could pick up an outfit here to fit right in at the rodeo, night club, or a concert for San Jose's legendary norteño band, Los Tigres del Norte.

While the members of this Grammy and Latin Grammy award-winning band were born in Sinaloa, they got their

---

Saddle up to watch fearless wranglers take on bucking broncos at Rancho Grande de Morgan Hill and the annual Gilroy Rodeo.

One-stop-shop for ice cream and Western wear at El Nuevo Rancho Grande.

start in San Jose in the 1970s and have lived here for more than 40 years. The internationally known band has sold millions of records with songs sharing the migrant experience in the United States, criticizing anti-Mexican racism, and celebrating the courage of the immigrants who have built and continue to shape our community.

BOOTS & MORE

What: El Rancho Nuevo Grande

Where: 1539 Alum Rock Ave.

Cost: Prices vary. Clothing and boots range from budget to higher-end brands.

Pro Tip: Try the "mangonada," mango ice cream with a generous scoop of fresh mangos, a swirl of sour-sweet chamoy sauce, and a sprinkling of chili lime salt.

RAISING THE DEAD

What psychedelic rock legends played their first show in San Jose?

San Jose was the birthplace of the Grateful Dead. While the band had been performing together for a few months under different names, their first show and public launch as the Grateful Dead happened on December 4, 1965, at a house party near San Jose State. This coming out was also the first public Acid Test, a series of parties organized around the use of the psychedelic drug LSD, organized by Beat Generation author Ken Kesey. This melding of a psychoactive experience with music influenced the Grateful Dead's sound and passionate and collective community of touring fans that they built over the years.

While the band had attended Kesey's first Acid Test in Soquel the week before, that was a small and private event. The party in San Jose was bigger and open to the public. To get the word out, Kesey had gone to San Jose Civic Auditorium that night to hand out flyers as people left a Rolling Stones concert. (He apparently invited Mick Jagger and Keith Richards, but neither of them showed.) Concertgoers walked over to the old Victorian home and lined up to pay $1 to get into this legendary after-party.

Beat legend and member of Ken Kesey's Merry Band of Pranksters, Neal Cassady lived with his wife, Carolyn, at 1047 E. Santa Clara St. in the 1950s. Their friends, Jack Kerouac and Allen Ginsberg, were known to come down for parties in the South Bay and crash with them for several weeks at a time.

The San Jose home where, in 1965, a recently formed local band played their first show as "The Grateful Dead."

LONG STRANGE TRIP

What: The Victorian house where the Grateful Dead played their first show.

Where: 635 E. St. James St.

Cost: Free, private residence. Do not disturb.

Pro Tip: The house was originally located near Santa Clara and 5th Streets, but it was moved to the current location on St. James Street during construction of San Jose City Hall.

While the Rolling Stones never turned out for this show, Jann Wenner, founder of *Rolling Stone* magazine, was in the crowd that night. The magazine featured the Grateful Dead in their first issue two years later.

A later resident of the home, local musician Ron Cook, filled the basement walls with sand to block out sound and used it as a hangout and recording space hosting San Jose's very own Doobie Brothers (while they were living nearby at 285 S. 12th St.), Stevie Nicks from Fleetwood Mac (then a student at San Jose State), and Skip Spence, one-time member of Jefferson Airplane.

GUIDED BY GUILT?

What's the real story behind San Jose's strangest house?

Anyone who has lived in or visited San Jose knows the story of our most famous, and certainly not secret, oddity. Sarah Lockwood Winchester was a wealthy Connecticut widow overcome by grief after the loss of her husband and infant child. She sought guidance from a psychic who told her to move west and build a house nonstop for the rest of her life to appease the spirits that haunted her. It was said that these spirits were the ghosts of those killed by the Winchester rifle, the weapon that brought her great fortune. Over the next 38 years, Winchester built a sprawling 24,000-square-foot and 160-room mansion, riddled with strange architectural features, such as doors that open to blank walls and second-story drop-offs, and staircases that lead straight into the ceiling.

But was this strange house really the product of a haunted and guilt-ridden soul?

Historians and people who knew her say there's little evidence for these legends and suggest instead that Winchester was a private person targeted by the sensationalist media of the day. These flashy narratives were further exaggerated by the amusement park builders who acquired the home and opened it up for "house of mystery" tours just months after she passed.

While it wouldn't have been unusual for Sarah Winchester to have visited a psychic medium since spiritualism was popular among women of her social class at the time, there is no evidence that she ever saw a medium or was interested in the occult.

An aerial view of Winchester's sprawling 160-room mansion.
Photo courtesy of the Winchester Mystery House

Historians point to how Winchester was an avid but self-taught architect. She saw the house, one of several she owned in the Bay Area, as her "hobby house," a place where she could experiment with new styles, ideas, and methods. She never worked from a centralized plan and lacked formal education in design, which could account for the eclectic construction and projects that just didn't work. Correspondence shows she often took extended breaks from construction for months at a time, especially after the Great 1906 earthquake, which caused severe damage to the house. She was heartbroken by this loss and chose not to rebuild portions, choosing instead to just clear the rubble, admitting once that the house now "looked as though it had been built by a crazy person."

Haunted or not, it's worth seeing Winchester's quirky labor of love in person on a guided tour.

SARAH'S PLACE

What: Winchester Mystery House

Where: 525 S. Winchester Blvd.

Cost: $20 and up

Pro Tip: Special events for Halloween, Friday the 13th, and Christmas. Already been? The "Explore More" tours visit areas not previously open to the public.

SACRED SECRETS

Who are the Rosicrucians?

For most San Joseans, Rosicrucian Park is synonymous with the Rosicrucian Egyptian Museum, a kid-friendly local museum that offers the largest collection of Egyptian, Babylonian, and Assyrian artifacts west of the Mississippi—3,000-year-old mummies, ornate coffins, scrolls, tablets, shrouds, scarabs, jewelry, amulets, a model of the Tower of Babel, and a replica of an Egyptian noble's tomb. It is a great place to learn about Egypt, but why exactly is this museum here?

The Rosicrucian Order Ancient and Mystical Order Rosæ Crucis (AMORC) is a secretive fraternal organization that believes that their members hold lost wisdom passed down to them from ancient Egypt. The San Jose Grand Lodge serves as one of the world's headquarters for the organization and is the clearinghouse for their English-language media including print mailings, YouTube channel, and podcast.

Harvey Spencer Lewis, a New Yorker who was initiated into Rosicrucianism on a trip to France, brought the order to California in the early 20th century with a mission to spread the beliefs across the English-speaking world. The philosophy took hold here, as this was at a time when many people were experimenting with alternative spiritual and metaphysical beliefs. Lewis bought land in the Rose Garden neighborhood and set up Rosicrucian Park. Over the next decade, the community built the Egyptian Museum, a planetarium, a

Rosicrucians believe mathematician Isaac Newton may have been a member because he had a large collection of alchemy books that he kept hidden; this wasn't considered acceptable for a serious scientist.

The Rosicrucian Egyptian Museum has the largest collection of Egyptian artifacts on display in western North America.

temple, a research library, and a Shrine, which houses the ashes of Lewis and other former top Rosicrucian officials. All buildings were inspired by ancient Egypt and Egyptian architecture.

Rosicrucians believe in metaphysical healing and organize the Council of Solace, a group that meets daily to meditate on behalf of sick and economically struggling community members at the park's temple. Additionally, Rosicrucians believe in alchemy, that there is a way to convert base metals, e.g., lead, into gold and gems through a mix of chemistry and mental and spiritual belief.

ANCIENT ALCHEMY

What: Rosicrucian Park

Where: 1342 Naglee Ave.

Cost: The grounds, including a labyrinth, research library, and meditation sessions, are free. Admission to the Egyptian Museum is $9 with reduced prices for seniors, children, and students.

Pro Tip: You can join one of the AMORC community's free daily (Monday-Friday) Council of Solace Meditation sessions in the Grand Temple. Arrive early and ask the meditation leader for the specific protocol on how to enter and exit the central chamber.

TRULY HARTLESS

When did an angry mob take the law into their own hands?

One of the most infamous crimes in San Jose's history happened in 1933 in St. James Park. Brooke Hart, heir to the popular Hart's Department Store, was abducted on his way home from work and held for ransom. Police traced the ransom call to a phone booth right next to the police station, where they cornered the bumbling kidnapper, Thomas Thurmond, and soon after detained his stated accomplice, Jack Holmes. The pair soon confessed to having killed Hart by throwing him off the San Mateo Bridge and into San Francisco Bay. This case was detailed in the riveting true crime book, *Swift Justice: Murder & Vengeance In A California Town*, by former *Mercury News* columnist, Harry Farrell.

Once the body was found, a mob of 5,000 people gathered in St. James Park across from the Old Courthouse and county jail where the accused kidnappers were held. Members of the crowd battered down the door of the jail, dragged the two out of their cells and over to the park,

MOB TOWN

What: Site of the infamous public lynching of two men accused of kidnapping a wealthy local businessman.

Where: St. James Park

Cost: Free

Pro Tip: Nearby Hart's Dog Park (194 W. Santa Clara St.) has a mural inspired by the Hart Department Store's logo.

The city cut down the elm and mulberry trees where Holmes and Thurmond were hanged shortly after the lynching. Locals saved branches and kept them as morbid souvenirs.

One of the original warehouses for Hart's Department Store, a popular downtown department store. At the time of his death, Brooke Hart was vice president of the company and was being groomed to take over the family business.

and hung them up in two trees. Members of the mob took turns attacking the men and stripped off their clothes to further humiliate them. Though never publicly named, prominent members of the community were said to have been spotted waiting in line to take a hit.

While many locals considered this attack on two people who hadn't yet been tried and convicted a miscarriage of justice and stain on the city, many at the time supported the lynchers, including California's governor, James Rolf, who called the mob "patriotic" and promised that no one would ever be prosecuted for it. While not racially motivated (Hart, Holmes, and Thurmond were all white), the attack spread fear among San Jose's diverse community, which believed that, even if wrongfully accused, a similar thing could happen to them.

THAT'S ELECTRIC

What local landmark was said to have inspired the Eiffel Tower?

Always looking for ways to stand out and advance our technological progress, San Jose became the first city west of the Rockies to have electric streetlights. The idea spearheaded by the editor of the *San Jose Daily Mercury*, J.J. Owens, was to be novel and a source of urban pride for the growing city. Uniquely, this city infrastructure was provided by a single 237-foot triangular steel light tower that spanned the intersection of Market and Santa Clara Streets.

The ambitious project was striking, but it had some issues. The lights were not mounted in a way that would efficiently illuminate the street. Most of the light was directed out and away from the city and toward the sky. And the police complained that drunken revelers would climb it after the bars closed. Despite these issues, the tower became an iconic symbol of San Jose, decorated for the holidays and featured on postcards shared around the world.

After a few decades, the tower fell into disrepair and was badly damaged in a windstorm in early 1915. Alex Hart, the founder of downtown's popular Hart's Department Store (and father of Brooke Hart, whose alleged killers were publicly lynched) had started a fundraising campaign to repair the San Jose symbol, but in the midst of this, another storm came through and caused the remaining fragments of the tower to come crashing down.

Farmers as far away as Los Gatos claimed that the artificial nighttime light prevented their chickens from laying eggs.

Visit History Park to see a replica of the electric light tower.

GET LIT

What: A half-size replica of the electric light tower that once stood at the corner of Market and Santa Clara Sts., lighting all of downtown San Jose.

Where: History Park, 635 Phelan Ave.

Cost: Free

Pro Tip: The documentary, "The Light Between Two Towers," shares the story of this San Jose icon and evidence for the alleged French connection.

Some people believe San Jose's light tower may have inspired the Eiffel Tower in Paris. The San Jose light tower predated the legendary Parisian tower and had some similar dimensions. The light tower was featured in international architectural publications that Eiffel's team of designers would have read. Additionally, a French-born San Jose resident named Pedro de Saisset personally sent word back to family in France who were involved in the Eiffel Tower's design.

BOOM TOWN

Why is McKinley's cannon filled with cement?

St. James Park was laid out in one of the early downtown city plans in 1848, but for the first few decades the space was a dusty lot used for public gatherings and the gruesome Sunday afternoon bear and bull fights that were popular during that era. In 1868, landscape architect and designer of New York City's Central Park, Frederick Law Olmsted, laid out the modern park design with radial walkways and tree-lined paths.

If you walk through the park today, you might have noticed the statue of US President William McKinley standing alongside a cannon. The statue marks the time McKinley came to San Jose in May 1901 and spoke from a pedestal on that very spot. Commercial interests in San Jose were strong, and the protectionist Republican president was very popular. The crowd piled the podium where he spoke with fresh flowers. Four months after his visit, President McKinley was assassinated, and a campaign started to erect a statue here in his memory.

Over the years, the statue was home to a few acts of violence. In 1918, a local German immigrant named George Koetzer was accused by a hateful nationalist group, Knights of Liberty, of making un-American remarks. His attackers tarred and feathered him and chained him to McKinley's cannon. In 1933, the statue watched over the gruesome mob lynching of the two men accused of killing Brooke Hart.

The Old County Courthouse (161 N. 1st St.) was built in 1866 to serve as the California State capitol building in a failed attempt to persuade the legislature to bring the capital back to its original location, San Jose.

The statue of President William McKinley has stood witness to a lot of drama over the years.

If you look closely at the statue, you'll see that the metal cannon is filled with a block of white concrete, which is there because of another "violent" night. On Halloween in 1932, some jokers packed flammable materials into the cannon, blowing out the windows of the county courthouse.

MCKINLEY MONUMENT

What: Statue of US President William McKinley

Where: St. James Park

Cost: Free

Pro Tip: The statue faces the Old Courthouse.

CRIMINAL OR CRUSADER?

Who was the bandit Tiburcio Vasquez?

Tiburcio Vasquez was a legendary outlaw and at one time the most wanted man in California. He had deep roots in the region. His great-grandfather had come north to California as part of the Anza expedition in 1776, and his grandfather (also named Tiburcio Vasquez) was the mayor of San Jose from 1802 to 1807. Though the younger Vasquez was from a respected family and educated at a military school, he got into trouble with the law when he was a teenager. Over the years, he robbed stores and stagecoaches, was implicated in one murder, and found responsible for a second—the robbery and killing of three people at a store in Tres Pinos, south of Hollister. With increasing bounties on his head, he traveled around the state hiding from the law, until one of his own associates accused him of having an affair with his wife and turned him into the police.

After finding him holed up at a ranch in Southern California, authorities brought Vasquez to San Jose for trial. He was convicted and hanged in front of hundreds of bystanders at the old jail near where the Superior Court building now stands (191 N. 1st St.). Famously cool and collected both at his sentencing and the time of his execution, the only word he spoke was "pronto!"

Vasquez himself excused his actions as retribution for discrimination against people of Mexican and Spanish descent in the aftermath of the Mexican–American War. To this day, many see Vasquez as a folk hero, akin to Robin Hood,

Local playwright Luis Valdez's work *Bandido!* focused on Vasquez's life, the Tres Pinos robbery, and his eventual capture.

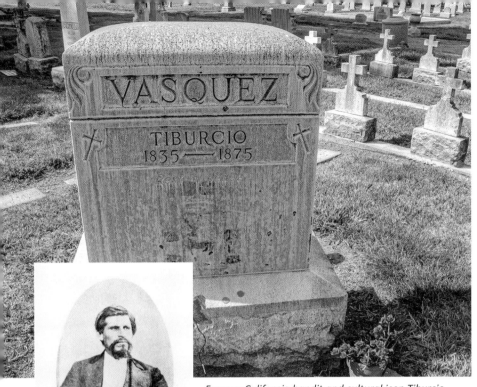

Famous California bandit and cultural icon Tiburcio Vasquez is buried at the Santa Clara Mission Cemetery.

Portrait of Tiburcio Vasquez around the time of his capture. Photo courtesy of University of Southern California Libraries and the California Historical Society

defending the oppressed and people who had their land and livelihoods stolen from them. Some of his writings show a sympathetic figure, and note that he instructed his men to use force only as a last resort. In one of his final interviews he had said, "I had numerous fights in defense of what I believed to be my rights and those of my countrymen. I believed we were unjustly deprived of the social rights that belonged to us."

ETERNAL REST

What: Santa Clara Mission Cemetery

Where: 490 Lincoln St., Santa Clara

Cost: Free

Pro Tip: Vasquez is buried in plot B-0673. Stop at the cemetery office to get a map and directions to this section.

ISLAND LIVING

What are "urban islands"?

If you look at a shaded map of San Jose, you'll notice that the city is not one contiguous shape. You'll see several little holes of land, or "urban islands" as city planners call them. These properties are not considered part of the city. The people who live in those neighborhoods do not live in the City of San Jose, they are not represented by a San Jose City Council member, and emergency dispatchers won't contact the San Jose Police Department if they call 911. In most cases, they are considered "unincorporated," with their public services managed by Santa Clara County.

One of the biggest urban islands is the community of Burbank. Almost 5,000 people live in this mostly unincorporated neighborhood near the intersection of Interstates 880 and 280. While many residents appreciate the unique character of their neighborhood, others say they didn't learn that their home wasn't actually in the City of San Jose until after they moved in.

How did these areas come to be? Most of San Jose's growth and development into California's third-largest city came by a massive campaign to annex neighboring small communities. After World War II, city leaders worked to incorporate outward in all directions, following the lead of quickly sprawling Los Angeles. San Jose's population grew from 95,000 in 1950 to 450,000 in 1970, and by then the once compact city covered 136 square miles. As San Jose city leaders encountered

There are more than a dozen unincorporated islands in the City of San Jose. The largest are in the Burbank, Alum Rock, and Cambrian neighborhoods.

The City of San Jose is dotted by "urban islands," unincorporated areas managed by Santa Clara County, but fully surrounded by city land.

neighborhoods where they couldn't convince locals to incorporate, they hopped over them, leading to these urban islands. During this time, downtown San Jose started to decline as the city's attention shifted outward.

While the city of San Jose still considers annexation in some cases, the city's primary growth strategy since the 1970s has been to grow up, promoting higher density development around transit centers and the revitalized downtown, rather than less sustainable and sprawling outward growth.

ISLAND HOPPING

What: There are several "urban islands" or unincorporated communities totally surrounded by the City of San Jose.

Where: Varies

Cost: Free

Pro Tip: To plug into the latest urban planning research and conversation, check out events hosted by the local office of SPUR, the San Francisco Bay Area Planning and Urban Research Association (76 S. 1st St., San Jose).

HOWDY, PARDNER

What local amusement park was inspired by Disneyland?

For almost 20 years, Frontier Village, a lush, tree-lined, Wild West–themed amusement park, delighted kids and families from across Northern California. Almost everyone who grew up in the South Bay in the 1960s and 1970s will share fond memories of the quirky amusement rides and reenactments of Wild West scenes. Located in South San Jose's Edenvale neighborhood, the park featured several rides and attractions that let visitors go back to the not-too-distant past when San Jose was a rough-and-tumble frontier town and launching pad for the Gold Rush. The park was inspired by the founder's family trip to Disneyland in its inaugural year and designed by a former Walt Disney Company designer. Visitors could wander the streets of the

GIDDYUP

What: Frontier Village birdhouses

Where: Edenvale Park, 200 Edenvale Ave.

Cost: Free

Pro Tip: Some of the birdhouses have been damaged or are in various states of disrepair, so catch them while you can. Inside the park's fence along Edenvale Ave. you can still see a segment of the old log fence that once surrounded Frontier Village.

Luna Park, once located near 13th Street and Highway 101, was San Jose's first amusement park, operating from 1911 to 1921. The business district there still bears the name along with the annual Luna Park Chalk Art Festival at nearby Backesto Park.

One of the Frontier Village birdhouses, part of an art installation marking the site of where the popular Western theme park's Old Railroad Station once was.

A decaying remnant of the old log fence that used to surround Frontier Village.

park's namesake village, watch staged cowboy shoot-outs, and ride a horse-drawn stagecoach, railroad, and a mine car.

Though the amusement park closed in 1980, the city later developed the property as Edenvale Gardens Regional Park. In 2007, artist Jon Rubin created a set of birdhouses in several areas of the park, mounted on the actual site of some of Frontier Village's most loved buildings and rides. Each pole has a plaque that shares historic photos of the amusement park and interpretive text as well as a listing of local bird species that might be drawn to these homes.

FIVE CHINATOWNS

Where can you learn about San Jose's lost Chinatowns?

After Chinese laborers were instrumental in building the Transcontinental Railroad, connecting the United States coast-to-coast, many of them came to California's growing cities to build a new life. They found many barriers, including laws preventing Chinese immigrants from obtaining business licenses, owning real estate, and interracial marriage. Even further, under the Expatriation Act, signed by President Theodore Roosevelt in 1907, American-born women who married a Chinese man could be stripped of their own US citizenship.

The Ku Klux Klan and other hate groups were on the rise and had active San Jose chapters. James D. Phelan, onetime mayor of San Francisco and US senator, ran his reelection campaign on a platform against "oriental aggression" and using the slogan "Keep California White" on his campaign posters.

In this atmosphere, the Chinese community stuck close to their neighborhood—"Chinatown." From 1870 to 1931, there were five different Chinatowns in San Jose. The first (and third) San Jose Chinatown on Market Street, where the Fairmont Hotel is today, was devastated by a fire in 1870, rebuilt, and then destroyed again in 1887. Suspiciously, the night of this second fire, the fire department's tank had only enough water to keep the fire from spreading to adjacent neighborhoods, leaving no water to save the buildings in Chinatown.

To commemorate the site of the burned Market Street Chinatown, there's a marker mounted on the southwest corner of the Fairmont Hotel at the intersection of Paseo De San Antonio and South Market Street.

A replica of the Ng Shing Gung temple, center of community life in the city's last Chinatown, Heinlenville.

TEMPLE TIME

What: Chinese American Historical Museum at Ng Shing Gung

Where: History Park, 1650 Senter Rd.

Cost: Free

Pro Tip: The museum is staffed by volunteers and only open the first and third Sundays of the month.

After this devastating fire, local businessman, John Heinlen, offered the community a parcel of land he owned on 6th Street between Jackson and Taylor Streets. The neighbors rebuilt, this time as a gated community (called "Heinlenville," the site of Japantown today) with barbed-wire fencing, fire-resistant brick buildings, and a nighttime security guard. Though the world outside was still a hateful mess, the community finally had the relative safety of their neighborhood, Chinese-owned businesses, and the community center—the Ng Shing Gung Temple (temple of the Five Sages), featuring a beautiful, gold-gilded altar.

Though the temple was eventually razed, the city kept the golden altar, furnishings, and part of the facade. In the 1980s a community group formed to fundraise to rebuild the temple for use as the Chinese American Historical Museum.

BUTTERFLY EFFECT

How did a volcanic eruption in the middle of the Atlantic Ocean shape San Jose?

On September 27, 1957, the earth started to tremble a quarter mile off the coast of Faial Island in the Azores, a Portuguese territory and archipelago in the middle of the Atlantic Ocean. Over the next 13 months, the Capelinhos Volcano erupted spewing volcanic ash, burying homes and killing off the vegetation that fed local livestock. Making things worse, a series of strong earthquakes hit the island in May 1958.

San Jose local, Joe Faria, was just a kid when this happened. His parents' business was damaged by the volcano, and their home was destroyed in the earthquake. He remembers people of the town gathering in an open space in the village center, praying all night that the island wouldn't sink into the ocean.

The Faria family left the islands and were sponsored by relatives already living in California under the Azorean Refugee Act sponsored by then US Senator John F. Kennedy. Ultimately, more than half of Faial's population fled the islands. Many came to San Jose, bringing local businesses and traditions that were common on the rural Catholic islands, such as the Festas do Espírito Santo (Festivals of the Holy Spirit), religious parades where they crown a queen from the community. These traditions are carried on today at the landmark Five Wounds Portuguese National Church and the annual Dia de Portugal festival.

Explore the main sites of "Little Portugal"— the stunning Five Wounds Portuguese National Church, Adega Restaurant, Popular Bakery, Trade Rite Portuguese Market, and Cafe Docanto.

An exhibit on village life in the Azores at the Portuguese Historical Museum in History Park.

Today, Joe Faria is retired and spends his time helping out at the Portuguese Historical Museum, which documents the stories of the Azores and their contributions to our local community. I ran into him while he was fixing a water pump to keep rain from flooding the museum's basement. He walked me around that subterranean floor, which displays exhibits about the Azorean village life his family once led and the eruption that brought them to San Jose.

ON ISLAND TIME

What: Portuguese Historical Museum

Where: History Park, 1650 Senter Rd.

Cost: Free

Pro Tip: The annual Dia de Portugal festival celebrates Portuguese history, dance, music, and food.

RESIST AND REMEMBER

Where can you learn about one of America's darkest chapters?

Around the corner from San Jose's historic Japantown business district, an unassuming museum takes on a critical mission. The Japanese American Museum of San Jose illuminates the experiences of families incarcerated by the US government during World War II. This program, issued by an Executive Order of President Franklin Delano Roosevelt in February 1942, forced more than 100,000 Japanese American residents of California, Washington, Oregon, and Arizona from their neighborhoods to harsh inland "relocation camps," where families lived in isolation for more than three years. Museum visitors can also learn about early emigration from Japan to America, Japanese leadership in California's agricultural industry,

NEVER AGAIN

What: Japanese American Museum of San Jose

Where: 535 N. 5th St.

Cost: $5-$8

Pro Tip: Just outside of the museum are some works of public art, including a sculpture of a family packed to leave and a copy of the public internment order once posted in San Jose's Japantown.

The Day of Remembrance marks the anniversary of the signing of Executive Order 9066. Each year, hundreds gather together for a candlelight vigil through Japantown to remember that great violation of civil rights and to reflect on the continued presence of racial violence and discrimination in America.

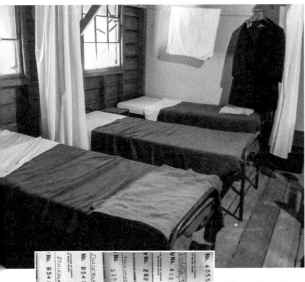

A replica of the spartan bunks Japanese American families lived in while incarcerated during World War II.

Name tags issued to interned families, in an exhibit at the Japanese American Museum of San Jose.

and some of the day-to-day challenges Japanese Americans faced building a life in California.

The museum shares photos, maps, and displays about life in the camps, including a haunting replica of one of the barracks, as well as stories about how the detention turned San Jose's Japantown into a ghost town, shuttering many family businesses and ripping children away from their schools and friends. Many of the stories are presented in the words of local community members, now neighborhood elders that were affected, including Norm Mineta, former US Secretary of Transportation, congressmember and mayor of San Jose.

POUND FOR POUND

How can you experience a Japanese New Year tradition?

Mochi is a sticky rice cake that's considered lucky in Japanese culture and traditionally eaten as the first meal of the New Year.

In generations past, Japanese American families would make this seasonal treat at home by steaming a big vat of rice, pounding it down by hand using a large wooden mallet, and then hand-shaping the paste into small, rounded cakes.

Starting in the 1960's, many families opted to skip this laborious process and buy their New Year's mochi at the Shuei-Do Manju Shop on Jackson Street in Japantown. This family-owned sweet shop wasn't able to keep up with the growing demand, so they asked a local Japantown church if they might be willing to start producing the rice cakes for the community.

Now, more than 40 years later, the Wesley United Methodist Church still hosts an annual, volunteer-led community mochi-making event, called a "mochitsuki" (derived from mochi, which means "rice cake" and tsuku, which means "to pound").

While the church volunteers no longer pound the rice by hand (they have a machine that does that), it's still quite a process. On one weekend in December 2019, more than 150 volunteers produced 2,000 pounds of mochi that they sold to the community.

At any time of year, stop into the Shuei-Do Manju Shop (217 Jackson St.), which has been producing mochi and sweet manju in Japantown for almost 70 years. They are made fresh daily and sell out fast, so go in the morning for the best selection.

Volunteers roll and cut sticky rice paste into flattened cakes called mochi. Photo courtesy of Ham Tran

One part of the event is Camp Mochi, an educational program for kids featuring a demonstration of the traditional method of hand-pounding the rice. Volunteer Ron Ogi has been working at the event for the last 30 years, and he said he loves sharing the custom with every new generation.

Both the mochitsuki and Camp Mochi are open to the public, and anyone who wants to learn about the tradition is encouraged to join.

MMM-MOCHI

What: Mochitsuki, the traditional pounding of mochi, a Japanese rice cake eaten on New Year's Day.

Where: Wesley United Methodist Church, 566 N. 5th St.

Cost: Free to help, price varies for the mochi

Pro Tip: The church hosts this event right after Christmas, and they sell the hand-packaged mochi through the last week of the year.

COLOR Y CULTURA

Where are San Jose's last remaining Chicano murals?

Not every work of art is lucky enough to sit in a museum protected by walls and guards. Sometimes, creative works that are valued by the community are hidden in plain sight. This has been the case with many beloved hand-painted murals representing San Jose's Chicano culture that grace the walls of neighborhood schools, health clinics, and even convenience stores.

In the early 1900s, Mexican artists like Diego Rivera and Jose Clemente Orozco used large public murals to show off important historical figures and social justice issues in a way that everyone, regardless of education or literacy, could understand. In the 1960s, Chicano artists adopted this tradition sharing stories on walls all across San Jose.

In 2018, a much loved East San Jose work, "Mural de la Raza," was painted over after the privately owned building changed hands.

STREET ART

What: A number of culturally significant murals by Chicano and Mexican artists.

Where: Various locations. You can spot some of the city-protected murals at Our Lady of Guadalupe Church, Las Casitas apartment complex, Washington Elementary School, Fisher Middle School, and San Antonio Elementary School.

Cost: Free

Pro Tip: To see a map of new and old mural art in San Jose, check out the Murals & Public art map at https://www.codeforsanjose.com/heartofthevalley/

For more modern murals, look to Powwowsanjose.com, an annual festival that pairs new and established mural artists to create work in our neighborhoods.

"La Medicina y La Comunidad," painted in 1990 by Mexican artist Gustavo Bernal, on the front of the Gardner Health Center on East Virginia Street.

This mural had stood on Story Road for more than 30 years and depicted important images in Mexican and American history from the great city of Tenochtitlan, the ancient capital of the Aztecs, and such figures as César Chávez and Dr. Martin Luther King, Jr. One local activist said, "Our entire history was basically on this wall."

Spurred on by this loss, in 2019 local citizens successfully petitioned for the city to recognize six remaining murals as historic landmarks. This will protect them from destruction without notice, but local activists encourage us all to pay attention to the murals that remain and appreciate the stories they tell.

One of the local treasures is a work called "La Medicina y La Comunidad," painted in 1990 by Mexican artist Gustavo Bernal, on the front of the Gardner Health Center on East Virginia Street. This mural depicts health-care providers alongside Aztec warriors, showing their fight as an act of heroism, too.

COMMUNITY KITCHEN

Where can you experience the sacred over a free meal?

If you've ever wondered about the striking golden dome-topped building you see perched in the Evergreen Hills, it's Sikh Gurdwara Sahib, a place of worship for members of the Sikh faith, a religion that started in the 15th century in Northern India's Punjab region.

The temple, or gurdwara (which means "door to the guru"), offers beautiful views of the Bay and lights of the valley at night. Built on a former apricot orchard, the San Jose location is the largest gurdwara in North America. Sikh families from across the Bay Area come each weekend to pray, connect with friends and family, and take Punjabi language and cultural classes. Visitors come to the gurdwara each weekend to enjoy the view, the Indian architecture, and another unique tradition—sharing a free meal.

"Langar" is the word for the gurdwara's community kitchen. All visitors are invited to sit down and have a free hot meal served by temple volunteers. This meal service was started by Guru Nanak, the founder of Sikhism, as an act of charity, and most gurdwaras around the world provide this service. The meal is always vegetarian. On a recent visit, I was offered a cup of lentil curry, a scoop of rice, a piece of flatbread, and sweet rice pudding. After taking a tray and your food, you will sit down on one of the mats laid on rows on

While the gurdwara is open seven days a week, Sunday is the busiest day to visit, where as many as 5,000 people will come to the gurdwara from dawn to dusk to eat, pray, and connect.

At Sikh Gurdwara Sahib in the Evergreen Hills.

the floor. A few tables are in the room, but they are reserved only for the elderly and those unable to sit on the floor.

SHARE THE SACRED

What: Sikh Gurdwara Sahib

Where: 3636 Gurdwara Ave.

Cost: Free; donations welcome

Pro Tip: The community welcomes visitors and provides information to guide you through appropriate etiquette, such as covering your head and taking off your shoes before entering the Main and Langar Halls. You can find a comprehensive list of tips on the gurdwara's website and on posters hanging throughout the campus.

CINEMA AND CHAI

Where can you watch an Indian blockbuster in a historic theater?

The Towne 3 Theater has seen a lot of changes over the years. When it opened in 1925, then called the Hester Theater, it showed silent films. In the 1970s, it started showing adult films before the city passed an ordinance banning X-rated entertainment within walking distance of schools. In 1990, it was purchased by Camera Theaters and showed independent and arthouse films.

More recently, the theater has gone through another change of owners and now shows South Indian movies, providing Silicon Valley's diverse community with a steady rotation of current films. In contrast to the more commonly known "Bollywood" films that are usually presented in Hindi, most of the Towne Theater's movies are voiced in the South Indian regional languages of Telegu, Tamil, and Malayalam, though all the films are shown

SWEET TIME

What: Towne 3 Cinemas

Where: 1433 The Alameda

Cost: Varies

Pro Tip: All shows on Wednesdays are discounted

This theater played a role in one of San Jose's most famous crimes, the 1933 kidnapping of Brooke Hart and mob lynching of the accused killers in St. James Park. The key alibi of defendant, Jack Holmes, was that he couldn't have been at the scene of the crime because he was at the Hester Theater with his wife and friends watching the *Three Little Pigs*.

The Towne Theater on The Alameda opened in 1925 and was originally called the Hester Theater.

The Towne Theater specializes in South Indian films and serves Indian sweet and savory treats— and popcorn.

with English subtitles. If you are new to Indian cinema, the movies are action packed and full of immersive and twisting plot lines. And they are long, sometimes three hours or more, and presented with a short intermission midway through.

The small box office sells a variety of fresh Indian baked goods, deep-fried snacks, such as samosas, and such beverages as hot chai tea and cans of bright blue and red Thums Up (that's the correct spelling), the leading cola brand in India.

LOW AND SLOW

How did colorful custom cars become part of San Jose's identity?

Car culture has always been big in San Jose, but no cars have been as influential as the lowriders, the sleek, custom-built, and colorful rides with lowered bodies and hydraulic lifts. From the 1970s on, these cars have been a steady presence on San Jose streets, and owners planned meetups at La Raza Park (Parque de La Raza de Paz, now a disc golf course south of Hellyer County Park) and the shopping centers at Story and King, followed by group rides to cruise "low and slow" around the valley. While the car culture has crossed ethnic and socioeconomic lines, the lowrider movement was a big part of the local Chicano community.

In 1977, three San Jose State students, Sonny Madrid, Larry Gonzalez, and David Nuñez, started *Lowrider* magazine, an influential publication documenting this culture. The founders all chipped in to publish the first edition, putting out 1,000 copies. Over the years, the magazine grew to be one of the country's best-selling automotive magazines. In the year 2000, the publication had an average monthly circulation of 210,000 copies. With the decline of the print media, the magazine's publisher announced in 2019 that *Lowrider* was going out of print but will continue online and across social media.

Still today, lowriders and community car clubs are big in San Jose, and you can see these beautiful rides on display at many local festivals and events.

Classic lowrider cars on display at the annual Tamale Festival in Gilroy.

From the beginning, *Lowrider* shared more than just cars. The founders had been student civil rights activists and they focused on issues that were important to the Chicano community, including politics and issues of social justice. The publication also funded a scholarship program for Latino students. Though the activism declined, the magazine always served as a voice for underrepresented communities and worked to challenge negative stereotypes of lowrider culture.

THE LOW DOWN

What: The commercial parking lots near this intersection have served as longtime meetup sites for lowrider and custom car enthusiasts.

Where: The intersection of King Rd. and Story Rd.

Cost: Free

Pro Tip: San Jose's annual Dia de Los Muertos ("Day of the Dead") festival features food, music, cultural arts, and car clubs showing off their colorful, long and low rides.

SLIP AND SLIDE

Where can you burn the backside off your chaps?

"DO YOU NOT LIKE YOUR TAILBONE? THEN COME HERE!!" This was a 5-star Yelp review left by Tremaine E., for the Evergreen neighborhood's Brigadoon Park. Those who grew up in the neighborhood share fond, if sometimes painful, childhood memories of the park's old-fashioned concrete slides.

CONCRETE KINGDOM

What: Brigadoon Park

Where: At the intersection of Brigadoon Way & Daniel Maloney Dr.

Cost: Free, plus cost of ER visit or ambulance ride

Pro Tip: Bring an old flattened cardboard box or look for one at the bottom of the slides. Wear long pants and long sleeves to protect from friction burns.

Need more encouragement? Here's what others had to say: "Have friends out of town visiting? Bored and broke and can't afford to do anything except go to a park? Wanna almost smash your face and eat the ground? If you answered yes to any of the above questions, then this is for you!" writes Maleah M., and "even though over the years I've gotten more bruises and scars and ambulance rides from this place, IT'S MY FAVORITE!!!" says Nikki F.

In addition to the concrete slides, the park also has a modern playground area, picnic tables, and barbecue pits. Every day, kids come to the park to speed down this free retro thrill ride with their behind protected

First-timers: don't try to slide without a cardboard box—it keeps your pants from burning off!

The concrete slides at Brigadoon Park.

only by a corrugated cardboard box. The slides are steep, especially the narrow one on the left, and not for the faint of heart.

In recent years, the city installed rubberized playground turf around the base of the slides, so you have a softer place to land.

SEA STRIKES

Where can you go bowling under the sea?

Bowling and the aquatic world are not two things that usually go together, but somehow it works at Uncle Buck's Fishbowl and Grill, a 12-lane bowling alley and restaurant. The alley is decorated to make it feel like you are underwater. Fish and sea life are suspended over the lane, and your bowling ball is spit back to you out of the mouth of a shark, octopus, or crocodile.

The unusual restaurant is a brand of national hunting and fishing gear retailer Bass Pro Shops, and it's connected to the San Jose store. The store is an adventure in itself, with murals of California landscapes including Yosemite National Park and the Bay Area's golden hills, stuffed game, such as deer and wild boar; and a massive 14,000-gallon aquarium, stocked with freshwater targets, such as sturgeon, small and largemouth bass, striped bass, catfish, and carp. Watch out for the animal tracks printed on the floor. Can you guess which animal left which tracks?

MARINE WORLD

What: Uncle Buck's Fishbowl and Grill

Where: 5160 Cherry Ave.

Cost: $32-$37 per hour for the lane plus shoe rental

Pro Tip: If you visit at noon on Saturday, you can watch the staff at neighboring Bass Pro Shop feed the fish in their giant aquarium.

For a more classic bowling experience, check out 4th St. Bowl (1441 4th St.) and their vintage cafe, a long-time local hangout and breakfast spot just north of Japantown.

Bowling under the sea at Uncle Buck's Fishbowl and Grill.

A helping hand—or eight!

The lines to get a lane at Uncle Buck's can be long, especially on weekends, and they don't take reservations, so come prepared to wait. But you can stop at the bar and grab a drink and enjoy the quirky atmosphere while you wait.

ROSICRUCIAN EGYPTIAN MUSEUM (page 52)

GRAYSTONE QUARRY (page 114)

CHICANO MURALS (page 74)

ALUM ROCK PARK (page 156)

SPEED CITY (page 104)

LAGUNA SECA (page 168)
Photo by Jordan Plotsky courtesy of Santa Clara Valley Open Space Authority.

FURCON (page 40)

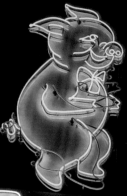

PURE
PORK
SAUSAGE

Stephen's
MEAT PRODUCTS

GET LIT (page 186)

WINCHESTER MYSTERY HOUSE (page 50)

BAY CHECKERSPOT BUTTERFLY (page 166)

MLK LIBRARY ART (page 10)

DUC VIEN BUDDHIST COMMUNITY PAGODA (page 14)

KNOX-GOODRICH BUILDING (page 116)

HART'S DOG PARK (page 54)

SPEED CITY

When was a silent protest heard around the world?

Nearly 50 years before San Francisco 49ers quarterback Colin Kaepernick took a knee at an NFL game to bring attention to racial inequality, two San Jose State track stars held up a fist on an Olympic podium to bring those same issues to the world stage.

In the 1950s and 1960s, San Jose was known as "Speed City," and San Jose State University had one of the best collegiate track programs in the country. Many African American athletes, recruited from rural areas around California, formed a tightly connected community that helped support each other in a city that was increasingly segregated and where Black residents were locked out of much of the housing due to racially restrictive covenants.

In the 1960s, in the wake of the assassination of Martin Luther King, Jr. and riots around the country, San Jose became a hotbed of civil rights activism. As the 1968 Olympic Games in Mexico City approached, many activists called for student athletes to boycott the games. While the boycott failed to pick up traction, some athletes decided to take the platform and protest individually.

During the medal ceremony for the 200-meter sprint, two San Jose State teammates, gold medalist Tommie Smith and bronze medal winner John Carlos, stepped onto the podium, shoeless and wearing black socks to represent Black poverty

To support Black student athletes who couldn't find housing, fellow athlete Charles Alexander organized a shared home they called the "Good Brothers Pad" (1065 N. 5th St.). Alexander's father prepared meals, and no one was ever turned away.

The statue Victory Salute *pays tribute to a heroic protest in defense of civil rights.*

in America. Both athletes closed their eyes, bowed their heads, and raised their fists to the roar of cheering crowds.

The International Olympic Committee called the protest "outrageous" and sent the star athletes back to San Jose, where they were blacklisted from future competitions and received death threats.

Smith and Carlos were eventually recognized for their courageous act and inducted into the US Track and Field Hall of Fame. In 2005, SJSU erected a 23-foot-tall sculpture of the two athletes on the podium in the center of the campus. The statue continues to honor the struggle for racial justice by serving as a gathering place for student demonstrations, including the 2020 protests in the wake of the police killing of George Floyd.

STAND UP

What: Statue honoring SJSU alums Tommie Smith and John Carlos's courageous protest at the 1968 Olympics

Where: Washington Square, on the campus of San Jose State University.

Cost: Free

Pro Tip: Park in the public garage on the corner of 4th across from the MLK Library.

CHOMP CHAMPIONS

How many hot dogs can you eat in 10 minutes?

Everyone knows about San Jose's love of pro sports, especially the Sharks and Earthquakes. But there's one lesser-known athletic circuit where San Jose locals have been unusually successful: competitive eating.

Two of the world's most famous competitive eaters hail from San Jose: Joey Chestnut and Matt Stonie. Joey Chestnut is currently the number one ranked competitive eater and "the greatest eater in history," according to Major League Eating, an organization that ranks competitive eaters and promotes food challenges, including Nathan's Famous Hot Dog Eating Contest in Coney Island, New York. Chestnut has won this contest 13 times in the last 14 years, eating 75 hot dogs with buns in 10 minutes in 2020.

Matt Stonie, the number three ranked competitive eater, got started while (ironically?) studying nutrition at Mission College in Santa Clara. He narrowly beat Chestnut in the 2015 Nathan's contest, breaking his eight-year reign. Stonie holds world records in more than a dozen other challenges, including eating 10 pounds of spaghetti and red sauce in eight minutes, 182 strips of bacon in five minutes, and 255 marshmallow Peeps in five minutes.

In between professional contests, both men share videos of their unusual eating challenges on their respective YouTube channels. Stonie has been particularly successful there, growing

Channel your own world champion by trying Mori Kitchen's Giant Ramen Challenge, Amato's Cheese Steaks 24-inch Cheese Steak Challenge, or the Smoke Eaters' Hellfire Challenge.

The Iguanas Burritozilla Challenge invites local eaters to finish a five-pound, 18-inch burrito in one sitting.

an audience of more than 10 million subscribers who tune in to see what weird or enormous thing he'll eat next.

One downtown San Jose restaurant ignited both Chestnut and Stonie's love for competitive eating. Iguanas Burritozilla Challenge invites visitors to eat a five-pound, 18-inch burrito to win a free T-shirt. While simply completing this monster in one sitting is a feat unto itself, when Chestnut first finished it as an amateur eater and student at San Jose State University, he did it in only eight minutes. As pros, both he and Stonie have since completed the challenge in under two minutes.

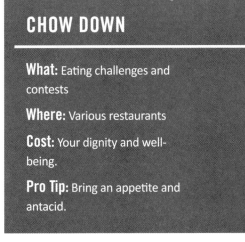

CHOW DOWN

What: Eating challenges and contests

Where: Various restaurants

Cost: Your dignity and well-being.

Pro Tip: Bring an appetite and antacid.

ROUND ABOUT

Where can you ride a bike at high speed with no brakes?

Perhaps the most unusual sporting venue in San Jose is located at Hellyer Park.

The Hellyer Park Velodrome is an arena for track cycling. It is the only cycling arena in Northern California and one of only 27 velodromes in the country. Built in 1963 for the Pan American Games, the velodrome later hosted the 1972 US Olympic Track Cycling Trials. Cyclists travel from all over to ride the track, train, and race.

ON TRACK

What: Hellyer Velodrome

Where: Hellyer County Park, 995 Hellyer Ave.

Cost: $10 and up, adults. Juniors age 9-18 are free with parent supervision. You must pay the county park fee to arrive by car.

Pro Tip: All of the races (usually held Wednesday nights) are open to the public to view for free.

Because of the rarity of these facilities, track cycling is a lesser-known corner of the cycling world, but it has some interesting characteristics. Track cyclists use only fixed gear, single-speed bikes without hand brakes. Riders take advantage of the arena's angled ("banked") track to moderate their speed, slow, and stop. These lightweight bikes plus the smooth, angled track let racers pick up much more speed than they can on a road or trail.

Most riders are drawn by the opportunity for speed that the track offers, and others like being able to cycle without the normal fears, such as potholes, dogs, and cars.

Weekly track races are free to watch. Photo courtesy of Hellyer County Park Velodrome

Racers come from across the state to train at Northern California's only velodrome, track cycling arena. Photo courtesy of Hellyer County Park Velodrome

To introduce new riders to the sport, every Saturday experienced cyclists lead a beginner's workshop covering everything you need to know to ride the track safely. If you don't have a fixed-gear bike, you can rent one there.

ON THIN ICE

Where can you go to skate like an Olympic legend?

For a city that rarely freezes, San Jose has turned out many Olympic medalists and star figure skaters. Kristi Yamaguchi, Brian Boitano, Peggy Fleming, Rudy Galindo, Debi Thomas, and Polina Edmunds all got their start skating in the South Bay.

And many locals eat, sleep, and breathe for the National Hockey League's San Jose Sharks and their minor league hockey affiliate, the San Jose Barracuda.

The local home base for this ice skating mania is San Jose's Solar4America Ice, the largest ice rink in the western United States. The complex serves as the training facility for the Sharks, the Barracuda, and several of the figure skating stars mentioned above. Along with their two affiliated rinks (in Fremont and Oakland), the organization hosts America's largest adult hockey league with more than 4,300 members.

If you want to learn how to skate like the pros, the facility offers open public skating times and competition figure skating

ON THE RINK

What: Solar4America Ice

Where: 1500 S. 10th St.

Cost: Admission starts at $8.50 and up, plus skate rental, if needed.

Pro Tip: Grab a drink or a meal at the ice rink's on-site pub, Stanley's Sports Bar.

A recently approved expansion plan will make it the largest ice facility under one roof west of the Mississippi River.

Skate where Olympic legends train at Solar4America Ice, the largest ice rink in the western United States.

and hockey organizations for all ages. In addition, they can match you up with a trainer or team for more unusual ice-based sports, such as broomball, curling, speed skating, and ice dancing.

KRAZY GEORGE

What legendary cheerleader invented The Wave?

One local personality loves San Jose and loves making crowds happy. "Krazy" George Henderson is a professional cheerleader who got his start in 1968 as a San Jose State student banging a drum, dancing, and making the crowds chant and cheer at SJSU football games. In 1974, he cheered at the first San Jose Earthquakes (Major League Soccer) game and was hired by the Kansas City Chiefs to come for the next season. Over the years he has worked for 20 different teams, banging his drum and getting crowds fired up.

Krazy George has made a few krazy claims over the years. He claims to be the first professional cheerleader (not true; a few NFL teams, such as the Baltimore Colts and the Dallas Cowboys, had paid cheerleading squads before he got started). He also claims to be the world's most famous cheerleader (possibly true; he estimates that over the last 40 years he has appeared in front of 25 million fans and has been seen by hundreds of millions of viewers on TV).

But his most important claim to fame is that he invented the world-renowned stadium cheer, "The Wave." While he dreamed

WAVE AT ME

What: "The Wave"

Where: Stadiums everywhere

Cost: Varies

Pro Tip: You can go to a San Jose State football game at CEFCU Stadium (1257 S. 10th St.) or San Jose Earthquakes game at Avaya Stadium (1123 Coleman Ave.).

In a 2019 interview, Henderson said, "As long as I can walk and carry a drum. Have drum will travel! I will be there because it's fun, and I love what I do."

One of San Jose's biggest sports fans, Krazy George Henderson.
Photo courtesy of Krazy George Henderson

it up at a San Jose State football game, the first time he brought it live to a crowd was at the nationally televised Oakland A's versus New York Yankees game in Oakland on October 15, 1981. The University of Washington Huskies have contested this claim and said they invented it at a home game against Stanford, but that game was two weeks after Henderson was captured on camera leading the crowd in Oakland.

Regardless of what he did or didn't do, his enthusiasm is contagious, and he lives to make fans feel that they are part of the game. To this day, Henderson continues to go to San Jose State games whenever he can.

ROCKING OUT

What gives Stanford University's campus that golden glow?

If you've ever visited Stanford University, you've probably admired the historic quadrangle made of golden sandstone and red-tiled roofs. Relative to other historic university campuses, Stanford feels particularly warm and inviting.

That unique golden stone came from the inappropriately named Graystone Quarry in the Santa Teresa Hills (it's not gray). The stone was shipped directly to Leland Stanford, founder of the university and president of the Southern Pacific Railroad, on a private rail spur he built just for the project.

The quarry was owned by Levi Goodrich, one of the first licensed architects in California, Goodrich had spotted the stone outcrops in the hills and identified them as a valuable and attractive building resource. He used the quarry for several of his own projects and sold it to others for the construction of Lick Observatory and the Carson City Mint in Nevada.

If you drive down Graystone Lane off of Camden Avenue today, you'll still see massive sandstone boulders and rocky outcrops towering over the residential subdivisions.

AT THE SOURCE

What: Site where glowing golden sandstone was mined and used to build the historic core of Stanford University, Lick Observatory, and the San Jose Museum of Art.

Where: At the intersection of Graystone Lane & Pfeiffer Ranch Rd., you'll see an old stone shed dating from around 1875 and a historic plaque.

Cost: Free

Pro Tip: Look to the hills of this area to see rocky outcrops, unique to this part of San Jose.

The San Jose Museum of Art, built as the original downtown post office, was one of architect Levi Goodrich's designs using this local sandstone.

An old shed still stands from the original stone quarry, at the intersection of Graystone Lane & Pfeiffer Ranch Road.

Architect Levi Goodrich designed many of San Jose's historic buildings, including the original downtown post office (now the San Jose Museum of Art), the Old Santa Clara County Courthouse, and the original campus of San Jose State University.

PUBLIC DEFENDER

What local attorney fought for women's rights and a fair legal system?

When you read a little bit about San Jose's history, it starts to feel that everyone in the city in the 19th century was an attorney. There was a lot of legal work to go around in the fast-growing city with so many residents and newcomers dealing with property disputes and setting up businesses. It was a good place for a lawyer to come and get rich.

Clara Foltz, an advocate for women's suffrage and the first female lawyer in California, became interested in law, both as a way to support her family here in San Jose—she was a single mom supporting five kids—as well as a way to fight for equal rights for women.

Foltz fought for the right to practice law herself and drafted the bill that changed the legal requirement for being a lawyer in California from being just for "white males" to being "any citizen or person." She lobbied for her bill at the state legislature and got the governor to sign it into law in 1878. After being denied admission to the newly established Hastings College of Law, she and her friend Laura Gordon (the second female lawyer in California), sued the school for discriminating on the basis of gender and won.

The Knox-Goodrich building (34-36 S. 1st St.) was owned by Clara Foltz's friend and fellow suffragist, Sarah Knox-Goodrich. Foltz rented her first office space from Knox-Goodrich in the "Knox Block," formerly located on the corner of 1st and Santa Clara.

The Santa Clara County Courthouse across from St. James Park.

Her biggest legacy may be in the work she did to make the legal system more humane and justice truly for all. Foltz was the first person in America to support the idea of the public defender—that the government should provide an attorney for people who can't afford to hire one on their own. She wrote and lobbied for this bill, and the state legislature passed the "Foltz Defender Bill" in 1921, guaranteeing that everyone in California accused of a crime would be granted an attorney.

JUSTICE FOR ALL

What: Where Clara Foltz, California's first female lawyer, tried her first cases.

Where: Old Courthouse, 161 N. 1st St.

Cost: Free

Pro Tip: In 1992, during the restoration after the Loma Prieta earthquake, construction workers discovered a long-forgotten dungeon beneath the old courthouse --two high security jail cells hidden behind a brick wall that was added at some point in the building's history.

IN STORAGE

What foundational computer tech was invented in San Jose?

Before the mid-1950s, using a computer was a daunting and physical task. Computers were room-size machines, and data was "saved" to a series of punch cards that users had to sort and run through the machine to make calculations and compile results. If you wanted to change an entry, you would have to re-sort the cards and feed them through the machine again manually. This process was slow, and results could take hours or even days.

IBM's first West Coast research and development facility, a small lab in downtown San Jose, upended this system with the IBM 305 RAMAC, the first computer to use a magnetic disk drive for data storage. The US Air Force had asked the company to design a random access inventory system, so IBM tasked 50 researchers with finding a way to store information on physical disks and access it quickly.

IBM rented a storefront building at 99 Notre Dame Ave. in downtown San Jose and used it as their first West Coast research lab from 1952 until the company built their large south San Jose campus. The San Jose Research and Development Laboratory had about 30 staff engineers, recruited from the Bay Area's top engineering schools. The lab was tasked with work on new, innovative technologies, different than anything their teams were working on back East.

Their refrigerator-size 350 Disk Storage unit was the predecessor of every hard drive that has been made since, including the domino-size drive that's in your laptop right now. This storage system made information instantly available and gave users the ability to find data quickly, edit it or erase it, and move it to various places in just seconds.

The downtown San Jose building where IBM designed the first magnetic hard drive.

This system helped to eliminate the pesky punch cards and let organizations think about data in new ways, including relational databases, the structure that is at the foundation of much of the software and applications that we use today on our laptops and smartphones.

SAVE THIS

What: The building where the first computer hard drive was invented.

Where: 99 Notre Dame Ave.

Cost: Free

Pro Tip: Learn more about tech history and see exhibits on the IBM 305 RAMAC at the Computer History Museum (1401 N. Shoreline Blvd., Mountain View).

To learn about another local innovation that brought us today's pocket-sized computers, visit the Intel Museum (2200 Mission College Blvd., Santa Clara) for exhibits on the company's history and the evolution of the microprocessor.

ON THE AIR

Where was the world's first radio station?

Long before our region became known as Silicon Valley, local engineers were experimenting with and making advances in another type of essential wireless technology—radio.

In 1909, Charles ("Doc") Herrold ran Herrold's College of Wireless and Engineering, an early technical training school that rented space in the Garden City Bank at the corner of First and San Fernando Streets. He and his students experimented with the new technology that was emerging at the time called "radio telephony." The building was seven stories tall and San Jose's first skyscraper. This gave them a good vantage point for these experiments, and they were able to transmit their first wireless voice signal for more than 20 miles, exciting the operators they had stationed in the region who heard their voices ring through.

After establishing that they could send voices across the airwaves, in 1910 Herrod began scheduling regular broadcasts of music and news on a show he called *San Jose Calling*. Later, the world's first broadcast radio network became KQW and then eventually KCBS, which broadcasts today at as 740AM, now based in San Francisco.

Charles "Doc" Herrold was born in the Midwest, but grew up in San Jose and studied at Stanford University. In 1900, he established a technical manufacturing company in San Francisco, but lost everything in the Great 1906 Earthquake.

While the seven-story Garden City Bank building was replaced in 1988 with a modern 17-story structure, another important media outlet now occupies the same site, KQED, the Bay Area's National Public Radio affiliate.

WORLD'S FIRST BROADCASTING STATION

FN — 1909   KQW — 1921   KCBS — 1949

ON THIS SITE IN 1909, CHARLES D. HERROLD FOUNDED
A VOICE RADIO STATION WHICH OPENED THE DOOR TO
ELECTRONIC MASS COMMUNICATION. HE CONCEIVED THE
IDEA OF "BROADCASTING" TO THE PUBLIC, AND HIS STATION,
THE WORLD'S FIRST, HAS NOW SERVED NORTHERN CALIFORNIA
FOR HALF A CENTURY.

PLAQUE DEDICATED ON APRIL 3, 1959, THE GOLDEN ANNIVERSARY OF RADIO
BROADCASTING, BY SAN JOSE STATE COLLEGE UNDERGRADUATE CHAPTER OF
SIGMA DELTA CHI, IN COOPERATION WITH KCBS AND AMERICAN TRUST COMPANY.

The site where Charles Herrold founded the first broadcast radio station. Today the building is the San Jose office of Bay Area public radio station, KQED.

TUNE IN

What: Site of the world's first broadcast radio station.

Where: 50 W. San Fernando St.

Cost: Free

Pro Tip: There are two historic plaques on the wall to the right of the building's entrance.

After spending a few years teaching at a technical college in Stockton, he moved home to San Jose and opened the Herrold College of Wireless and Engineering in 1909.

As he described these early broadcasts sharing a mix of news and music, "we have given wireless phone concerts to amateur wireless men throughout the Santa Clara Valley."

In 1959, his former assistant, Ray Newby described his routine, "it was a religion for Prof Herrold to have his equipment ready every Wednesday night at nine o'clock. He would have his records ready, all laid out, and what he wanted to say. And the public or listeners, it became a habit for them to wait for it."

BEHIND THE VINES

How did beer and wine come to San Jose?

People have been making booze in San Jose for as long as there's been a San Jose. Wine historian Charles L. Sullivan called the Santa Clara Valley "America's original premium wine-growing region" because growers imported quality French grapes and started planting vineyards here even before the industry took root in Napa and Sonoma.

BOOZY PIONEERS

What: The ruins of the Old Almaden Winery, the oldest winery in California. And the J. Lohr Winery on the grounds of the old Fredericksburg Brewery.

Where: Almaden Winery Park (Chambertin Dr. and Treviso Ave.). And J. Lohr San Jose Wine Center (1000 Lenzen Ave.).

Cost: Free

Pro Tip: You can see remnants of one of the original Almaden winery buildings in Almaden Winery Park on the corner of Chambertin Dr. & Treviso Ave.

While Spanish padres at Mission Santa Clara produced the first sacramental wine in 1798, vineyards weren't common here until the 1850s. Local nursery owner Antoine Delmas imported the first French grapevines into the state in 1852. That same year Etienne Theé, another local Frenchman and wine pioneer, planted the first commercial European grape vineyard in the county, Almaden Vineyards. While Almaden Vineyards is no longer based in San Jose (it was bought by a Central Valley–based company), the brand still exists.

As you might guess, German immigrants brought beer brewing with them to San Jose. The most famous of San Jose's early breweries was the Fredericksburg Brewery founded in 1869 on Cinnabar St., right off The Alameda. By 1889, the company was producing almost 60,000 barrels a year, and they shipped the suds up and down the West Coast and even to Mexico. The brewery resembled a six-story German Rhine castle replete with tall spires and crenelated turrets. The

The last remaining structure of the Almaden Winery, on land that is now a city park (Almaden Winery Park).

castle became their iconic image and was used on all their labels and marketing materials.

The Fredericksburg Brewery didn't survive Prohibition, but after repeal, San Francisco–based Pacific Brewing and Malting Company bought the brand and started producing beer under the Fredericksburg label until the 1950s. In 1952, Falstaff Brewery bought out the property and brewed beer there until the 1970s.

Today, there's still fermentation happening on this site. In 1974, J. Lohr Vineyards moved here and has been producing and bottling wines ever since.

While Antoine Delmas can be thanked for introducing wine grapes to California, he also brought a less welcome import—the brown garden snail. Intended for food (escargot), they soon spread across the state, plaguing crops and home gardens ever since.

CUTTING 'COTS

Why was San Jose known as the Garden City?

The Santa Clara Valley was once one of the world's largest producers of fruit, especially apricots and prunes, but also peaches, pears, and cherries. Orchards filled the valley floor, and in the spring, people would drive from all over to see the trees in bloom and smell the perfumed air. The region was nicknamed the Valley of Heart's Delight, and San Jose was known as the Garden City. Those who grew up during that time share stories about working summers harvesting fruit and slicing apricots open to dry, or "cutting 'cots," as they say.

As San Jose was so far away from the lucrative food markets on the East Coast and in Europe, local growers and packagers developed new technologies to help preserve and package foods. The sulfur drying technique still used today to retain the vibrant color of dried apricots, peaches, and plums was invented by Henry W. Coe, namesake of the South County state park.

The San Jose Fruit Packing Company was the first fruit canning company in the valley. The company opened a large cannery on a triangular site bordered by Auzerais Avenue, Sunol Street, and Los Gatos Creek. At one time, it was the largest cannery in the world, shipping 6.6 million cans in 1895 alone. The company later became part of the California Packing Corporation (Calpak) whose most well-known brand was Del Monte, and the Auzerais plant became known as Del Monte

---

To visit one of the last stone fruit stands in the valley, check out Andy's Orchard (1615 Half Rd., Morgan Hill). In the summer, the farm hosts popular tasting events where you can sample dozens of rare and unusual fruits.

Trays of apricots drying in the open air at Andy's Orchard in Morgan Hill.

Plant #3. The plant remained one of the busiest packing facilities in the valley until it closed in 1999. Plant #3 workers claim to have invented fruit cocktail as a way to use up remaining fruit bits.

After the plant closed the land was redeveloped into a condominium community. The builder, retained several of Plant #3's architectural features, including the plant's external walls, an old conveyor belt that marks the gateway to the community, and the signature Del Monte water tower.

IN THE CAN

What: The site of the original San Jose Fruit Packing Company and later Del Monte Plant #3.

Where: Cannery Square at Monte Vista Condos on the intersection of Auzerais Ave. and Wright Place

Cost: Free. Private residences, do not disturb tenants.

Pro Tip: You can find a historic plaque where the Los Gatos Creek Trail crosses Auzerais Ave. and see historic structures, such as the old water tower, conveyor belt, and part of the old cannery's roof in a courtyard near the light rail tracks.

BEARDED BEAUTIES

Where can you see a field of flowers and a stunning view?

For just six weeks in April and May, Nola and Gary Prevost open up their private hilltop ranch and flower garden to visitors who want to come and enjoy the day surrounded by colorful bearded irises.

Nola's Iris Garden is one of the country's largest iris viewing gardens, with more than 2,000 rare and hard-to-find varieties of the flower. They invite photographers, artists, families, and dogs on leash to come up during the bloom season to enjoy the color. The garden has meandering paths, benches, and a covered deck offering scenic views of the neighboring hills and the valley below. The roaming cats, chickens, and stacks of farm gear on the periphery remind you that this is not an immaculately manicured public park, but rather, someone's home open to the public as a labor of love. So, please be polite and treat it as such.

The garden started out as a hobby and retirement project after Nola's favorite bearded iris grower, based in Willow Glen,

BLOOMING FUN

What: Nola's Iris Garden

Where: 4195 Sierra Rd.

Cost: Varies

Pro Tip: The garden is only open to the public in the spring. You can purchase more than 1,000 varieties of iris on their website year-round.

Just a few miles down the road, visit CharMarron Peony Nursery (5335 Sierra Rd.), a seasonal peony nursery selling more than 200 hard-to-find varieties of peony.

Colorful fields of irises at Nola's Iris Garden.

Nola's Iris Garden has more than 2,000 varieties of iris and is open to the public for the spring bloom.

went out of business, leaving a void in the area for local flower lovers. The Prevosts expanded their collection of irises and began selling them locally. See one you like? Many are available for sale on Nola's website. Order them there and she'll dig the rhizomes, the bulb-like root system, right out of the bed and ship it to you at the appropriate planting time for your area. In the Bay Area, this is usually July through September.

SWARM SITE

What's the buzz surrounding the San Jose airport?

A plaque dedicated to a small but vitally important part of California's agricultural history and present industry is hidden at the San Jose Airport.

In 1853, the first swarm of honeybees arrived on the West Coast. A Texan named Christopher A. Shelton bought 12 hives of bees from a vendor in Panama on the way to his new home in California. He transported those hives by ship to San Francisco and then by train and then mule to his farm at Rancho Potrero de Santa Clara, on the site where the airport now stands. Only one of the hives survived this daunting journey, but these hardy pollinators produced three successful swarms that year, and the bees were sold at market to other growers.

These bees, known as German black bees (*Apis mellifera mellifera*), soon spread across the state and later the West Coast. The descendants of these bees and the bee pollination industry became an essential part of California agriculture, helping to ensure a sustainable harvest of almonds, berries, and other fruit.

ARRIVALS GATE

What: A plaque marking the spot where honeybees came to the West Coast.

Where: 1701 Airport Blvd.

Cost: Free

Pro Tip: The marker is in front of the international terminal at Mineta San Jose International Airport. You cannot stop on this stretch of curb, so either park in one of the airport parking garages or just slow down to snap a pic as you drive by.

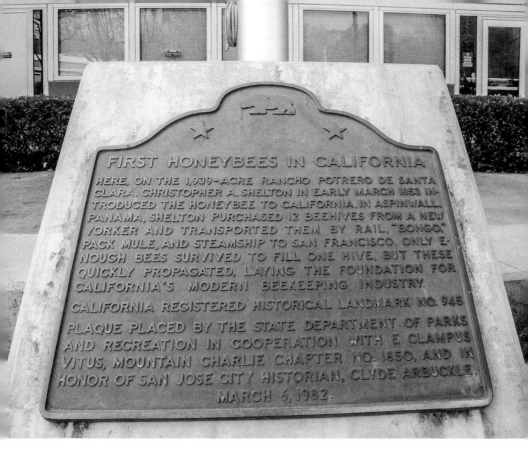

Historic marker sharing the site where honeybees were first brought to California by a local farmer. This land is now the site of the Mineta San Jose International Airport.

Honeybees helped shape California agriculture into a $100 billion a year industry that supplies more than half of America's fruits, vegetables, and nuts.

VARIED VEGGIES

How can you spice up your vegetable garden?

Bored with the starter vegetable selection at your big-box hardware store? Looking to diversify the foods you grow at home? Or are you craving a food you grew up with or were introduced to by family or friends and you want to try to grow it at home?

Check out Valley Verde, a local nonprofit that works to "empower communities through access to healthy and culturally preferred foods." The organization started during the 2008 recession as a way to help provide a low-cost and healthy source of fresh foods. They organized a home garden start-up and mentorship program, helping low-income families set up their first backyard garden and teaching them everything they needed to know to grow their own vegetables at home.

The second part of the mission, to provide "culturally preferred" foods, came about as they started to help families in their diverse San Jose community. In addition to the staple plants they were providing, such as lettuce, cucumbers, and tomatoes, participants said they wanted to include other vegetables and herbs that were important in their daily diets—for example, Mexican families wanted to grow tomatillos, chayote, and epazote, and Vietnamese families wanted to grow lemongrass and bitter melon. The program organizers realized there wasn't a good commercial source of starter plants for

Visit another urban farm nonprofit dedicated to healthy food access, Veggielution (Emma Prusch Park, 647 King Rd.) for their weekly produce stand every Saturday morning.

Valley Verde is a local nonprofit that helps community members set up home gardens and stock them with seedlings from food traditions around the world. Photo courtesy of Valley Verde

them, so they decided to grow the plants from seed themselves.

Today, the organization grows more than 40 different varieties, including many diverse and hard-to-find plants that they provide to their program participants for free and sell to local home gardeners. All proceeds go to support Valley Verde's home garden programs.

CURRY UP

What: Valley Verde Urban Farm & Greenhouse

Where: 321 Gifford Ave.

Cost: Varies

Pro Tip: To buy seedlings, visit their greenhouse (open Monday through Friday), place an order on their website, or go to the spring Seedling Market.

WHAT A TREAT

Where can you find a hidden ice cream factory?

One of the best local sweet treats is literally hidden in the back of a tiny parking lot off a residential street. It's easy to miss even if you're looking for it. You'll only know you are in the right place when you enter the lot and spot the vintage red-and-white sign.

Soon after Alfred Mauseth opened Treat Ice Cream on Santa Clara Street in 1951, customers started calling him, "Mr. Treat." At the time, the factory was right across the street from Roosevelt Junior High School, and kids would come over after school to buy ice cream cones. Today, the school is gone (replaced by Roosevelt Community Center and Park), and they no longer have a storefront on Santa Clara or sell ice cream by the scoop—only 1.5-quart plastic tubs that look much as they have for decades.

VINTAGE FREEZE

What: Treat Ice Cream

Where: 11 S. 19th St.

Cost: $7 for a 1.5-quart tub

Pro Tip: Open business hours Monday through Friday. Cash or check only.

Inside, you'll find a wholesale production factory with giant vats and a simple workbench that is the center of business, where you can order a tub to go. They offer dozens of flavors, including several unique and seasonal ones. Availability changes each week. Current flavors are always posted on the wall. One of their most popular flavors is the violet-tinted ube, made with purple yams from the Philippines.

You can go to the factory to pick up a tub or find it at local supermarkets, such as Zanotto's and Lunardi's.

Look for Treat Ice Cream at O'Brien's Ice Cream Parlor and Candy Shop at History Park.

Visit O'Brien's Ice Cream Parlor and Candy Shop (1650 Senter Rd.), a working replica of a popular downtown ice cream shop that operated from 1878 to 1956. When the original O'Brian's opened, it was the first place to serve ice cream and sodas west of Detroit. Today the shop sells Treat Ice Cream and a selection of old-fashioned candies.

133

NO WAFFLING

What childhood breakfast staple was invented in San Jose?

In 1936, Frank Dorsa and his two brothers, Sam and Anthony, started a food company that made premixed dry waffle batter in their parents' garage on Oak Street, south of downtown. Frank was an inventor, always looking out for other food innovations, and in 1938 bought a potato chip plant and invented an automatic continuous potato peeler.

In the 1950s, Frank invented a machine that could make thousands of waffles per hour, which made the mass production of frozen waffles possible. Customers started calling them "Eggos" because of the egg flavor, and the name stuck. In 1961, he built a waffle factory east of downtown San Jose on a street now named "Eggo Way."

The ability to make and sell a hot breakfast that's ready in just minutes was attractive in the convenience food, postwar era. In 1966, the Dorsa brothers sold to a company that was later acquired by global food giant, Kellogg. Kellogg introduced new breakfast product lines, such as microwave pancakes and French toast.

Stop into any Vietnamese bakery and order a pandan waffle. These green, Instagram-friendly waffles are made with pandan (a southeast Asian herb) and coconut milk and eaten plain. They are a common street food in Vietnam and a popular snack in San Jose. (Try: CD Bakery & Deli in Lion Plaza, 1816 Tully Rd., Suite 198)

Eggo waffles have been produced at this San Jose factory since it was built by the Dorsa Brothers in 1961.

Try another much-loved local sweet treat, pandan waffles, available at many local Vietnamese bakeries and sweets shops.

Eggo waffles and breakfast foods now come in almost 40 varieties, including flavored and kid-friendly cartoon-themed waffles. Today, they still produce several of them at the Eggo Way plant. The plant is surrounded by a high fence, and anyone seen poking around for photos will be visited by a friendly security guard trying to discern whether you intend to "Leggo his Eggo."

FROZEN TREATS

What: The Kellogg Company's San Jose plant produces a variety of Eggo products.

Where: 475 Eggo Way

Cost: Free

Pro Tip: The plant is gated, and public access is not allowed.

CHEESY FUN

What troupe of robotic entertainers got their start in San Jose?

Whether you think the robotic animals at Chuck E. Cheese family restaurant are creepy or cute, the one-of-a-kind franchise started right here in San Jose.

In 1977, Nolan Bushnell, a co-founder of Atari, got into the restaurant business and opened the first Pizza Time Theater in San Jose. This unique restaurant featured a band of singing and dancing robotic cartoon animals, led by a giant buck-toothed rat in a bowler cap named Chuck E. Cheese. These animatronic entertainers played music and cracked jokes while families noshed on pizza and played carnival-like arcade games.

The franchise, later renamed Chuck E. Cheese after the much-loved band leader, exploded, and today there are more than 600 locations around the world.

While the first Pizza Time Theater restaurant is no longer there, it stood on Winchester Boulevard where Santana Row shopping center is now. The modern chain has three locations in the South Bay, two in San Jose (2445 Fontaine Rd. and 1371 Kooser Rd.), and one in Cupertino (19805 Stevens Creek Blvd.).

Because kids today are less enthralled by '70s era robotics, the chain has announced they are planning to phase out Chuck and his band, so catch them while you can.

***

After college, Nolan Bushnell was unable to get his dream job working at Disney, but created Chuck E. Cheese to honor his hero.

Chuck E. Cheese, the namesake of the popular family restaurant chain that started in San Jose.

PIZZA TIME THEATER

What: Chuck E. Cheese

Where: 2445 Fontaine Rd.

Cost: Varies

Pro Tip: This Chuck E. Cheese location is said to be haunted by the ghosts of two children that died on the site. Visitors have claimed they can see a figure of a little girl and hear a young boy crying for his mom.

Chuck's merry band still performs at the Fontaine Rd. restaurant and entertainment center.

SCORNED LOVE

What was San Jose's most sordid love affair?

One name many San Joseans recognize is Henry Morris Naglee, a civil engineer and Civil War general turned orchardist and brandy distiller. In 1902, his downtown San Jose property was converted into San Jose's first residential subdivision, Naglee Park.

But this esteemed general was the target of San Jose's original revenge porn. A scorned lover published a book of all the private letters he wrote to her during wartime to show how he made repeated promises to her of his love and commitment.

In *The Love Life of Brigadier General Henry M. Naglee*, Naglee's former lover, Mary L. Schell, shared deeply personal letters that Naglee had written to her before they broke up. The book's preface explains what was to come. "All are seasoned with a 'passionate' flavor that cannot fail to tickle the palate of the most sensational epicure."

In letters that start "My darling baby," "enchantress," or "little love," Naglee pours his heart out about his fears and anxiety, illnesses he's suffering, including typhoid fever, and bitter disagreements with his supervisors, including the actions of President Lincoln. In the most scintillating exchange, he includes a hand-drawn nude drawing of himself doing push-ups in his bathtub every morning to show off how strong he

Naglee was once targeted by the Ku Klux Klan for supporting Chinese workers. In 1869, the KKK claimed they were behind a fire that damaged the Naglee Brandy Distillery.

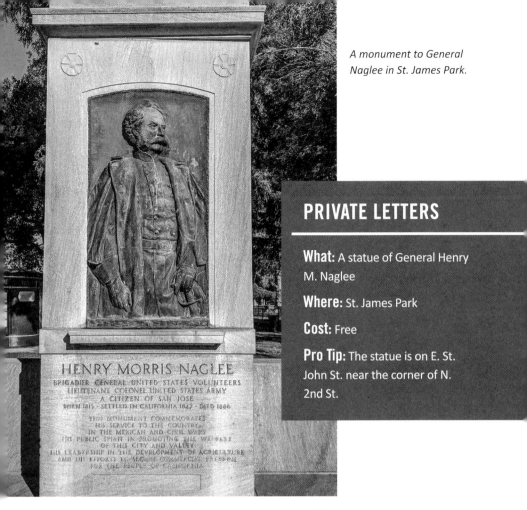

A monument to General Naglee in St. James Park.

PRIVATE LETTERS

What: A statue of General Henry M. Naglee

Where: St. James Park

Cost: Free

Pro Tip: The statue is on E. St. John St. near the corner of N. 2nd St.

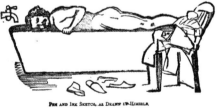

PEN AND INK SKETCH, AS DRAWN BY HIMSELF.

"Pen and ink sketch, as drawn by himself." The Love Life of Brigadier General Henry M. Naglee *by Mary L. Schell*

is. Another calls out, "Don't tell anyone, nor show our letters, will you, love?"

Naglee found his way into another scandal 12 years later after the death of his wife. His nanny at the time, Emily Hanks, filed a lawsuit against Naglee, claiming he proposed marriage and tried to seduce her.

HOT STUFF

What should you know before walking into that locally owned coffee shop?

A friend once told me about something that happened to her shortly after she moved to San Jose. "I had an appointment at the DMV but got there early, so I wanted to pick up a cup of coffee before I went in." Instead of stopping at the national chain, she looked up an independent coffee shop a few blocks away and walked over.

When she entered the dimly lit cafe, she found it full of older men, many smoking cigarettes, who turned to watch her come in. But the thing that surprised her was the server, a young woman in her 20s dressed only in a tiny bikini. She ordered her coffee to go and quickly hurried away, having discovered one of San Jose's seedy secrets.

These bikini or lingerie cafes are sometimes dubbed "Vietnamese cafes" or "Vietnamese coffee shops," named for their prevalence in Vietnamese enclaves in both San Jose and Orange County, California. In prewar Vietnam, male-oriented coffee shops were popular hangouts and the closest thing to a strip club in the conservative culture.

While some of these cafes started with waitresses who were provocatively but fully dressed, competition between cafes led to skimpier and more revealing clothing. About a dozen of these hangouts are scattered around San Jose, and while most of them are operating above board, at least one popular cafe closed down after being cited repeatedly for having nude waitresses.

SURPRISE!

What: Bikini cafes including Cafe Paradise

Where: 2400 Monterey Rd.

Cost: Varies

Pro Tip: Check out the reviews on Yelp to get a sense of what the place is like.

The food is good, but it's not the main attraction at Cafe Paradise, a bikini coffee shop and hookah lounge on Monterey Road.

While food is clearly not the main thing that draws people to these cafes, the Vietnamese iced coffee sipped all day by the regulars is likely to be quite good and many serve tasty small plate appetizers.

Love Spanish tapas bars and Japanese izakayas? Check out one of San Jose's quan nhậu, Vietnamese pubs with sharable plates of hearty food that pair well with a cold beer. Try Binh Minh Restaurant (1006 E. Santa Clara St.) for goat served every way and tiết canh ("blood pizza"), coagulated duck blood topped with offal.

SUPREMELY DELICIOUS

What local restaurant was started by a Supreme Master?

San Jose is home to an international religious organization that runs a popular downtown restaurant, the Vegetarian House.

Followers of the community's spiritual leader, Ching Hai, call her the Supreme Master. She developed a tradition she calls the Quan Yin method or "inner light and sound" meditation. Followers say her teachings draw features from all major religions (Christianity, Buddhism, Hinduism, Judaism, and Islam) and believe that she can communicate directly with God. Followers are encouraged to lead a totally vegan diet, abstain from alcohol and other intoxicants, and meditate for at least two and a half hours a day.

The South Bay is the US headquarters of the Supreme Master Ching Hai International Association, Ching Hai's Celestial Shop (where she sells an odd mix of jewelry, dog houses, and meditation supplies), and the group manages a private office and initiation center in Morgan Hill.

The sustainably sourced and GMO-free dishes at the Vegetarian House are excellent. Many voracious meat eaters agree. While the staff at the restaurant never proselytize, you're surrounded by information and religious curiosities, and they will answer questions if you ask. The lobby has a life-size portrait of the Supreme Master and is decorated with the Supreme Master's personal nature photography. There's a TV over the

Loving Hut, a successful vegan restaurant chain with more than 200 locations around the world, was started by the Supreme Master Ching Hai's association.

A portrait of the Supreme Master Ching Hai greets visitors at the Vegetarian House.

(nonalcoholic) bar that plays the association's satellite television network, Supreme Master TV, all day. The waiting area has a bookshelf where you can browse more than a dozen books by Ching Hai, including *Secrets to Effortless Spiritual Practice; Of God and Humans: Insights from Bible Stories*; and my personal favorite, *The Dogs in My Life*, which is "collectively written by Ten Lucky Canines," a book about Ching Hai, written in the voices of her many pet dogs.

COMFORT FOOD

What: Vegetarian House

Where: 520 E. Santa Clara St.

Cost: Varies

Pro Tip: Visit suprememastertv.com for 24/7 livestream (with subtitles in 16 languages) offering information on the Supreme Master, veganism, and climate change.

PAINTED LADIES

What sandwich shop doubles as an art gallery?

The Sourdough Eatery is a labyrinthine brick restaurant with several rooms, a sprawling outdoor patio, and some unique kitsch. All the walls are covered by owner Barbara Lenhart's own oil paintings, an unusual mix of cute baby animals, celebrity portraits, sexy pinup girls, and patriotic images.

Lenhart says her work is inspired by Hollywood, where she grew up (her father was a chef at the legendary Brown Derby restaurant) and Paris, where she danced for three years as part of the famous Folies-Bergère cabaret group. In the 1970s, she and her husband started the deli-style sandwich shop, and she funneled her creativity and love of celebrity and drama into her painting. President George H. W. Bush liked the portrait she painted for him so much that he invited her to the White House. She also presented portraits to President Clinton and then First Lady Hillary Clinton when they visited San Jose.

The deli-style menu with classic options like roast beef and pastrami hasn't changed in decades, and all sandwiches come with a pickle on the side. For dessert, you can order a slice of

LUNCH AND LINGER

What: Sourdough Eatery

Where: 848 N. 1st St.

Cost: Varies

Pro Tip: Cash only; an ATM is on-site.

The shop offers 20 different sandwiches made with their home-baked sourdough bread always served hot from the oven.

*Original paintings
line the walls of the
Sourdough Eatery.*

carrot cake. The resident café cat roams around the dining room and might join you for lunch.

They are only open during lunch hours Monday through Friday, and it gets busy with county staffers and people on jury duty at the neighboring county Civic Center complex.

MAIN SQUEEZE

Where can you get a hot dog in a building shaped like a giant orange?

Mark's Hot Dogs has been serving East San Jose since 1936, but what everyone remembers is the stand's distinctive round orange structure. The building was originally constructed in the 1920s to serve as an orange juice stand. Entrepreneur Frank Pohl built dozens of these distinctive "Giant Orange" juice stands and mounted them along highways in California. Travelers would stop and walk up to one of the windows to order a cup of freshly squeezed orange juice.

Pohl sold off many of the quirky juice stands before retiring, and, in 1947, Mark's Hot Dogs moved into one of the San Jose stands, then located on Alum Rock Ave. After the City of San Jose declared it a historic landmark in 1992, they moved the stand to its current location on Capitol Avenue. Today, this is one of the last Giant Oranges remaining in California.

Mark's offers a trip back in time with classic menu items that have stayed mostly the same since the shop's earliest days. Their simple menu is still displayed on a hand-painted sign—hot dogs (regular, polish dogs, or chili dogs), chili cheese fries, nachos, milkshakes, and ice cream floats.

The inside of the round structure has been restored and decorated with orange and white tiles. There are two seats inside at the counter and four more spacious tables out back.

ORANGE YOU GLAD

What: Mark's Hot Dogs

Where: 48 S. Capitol Ave.

Cost: Varies

Pro Tip: Try the chili cheese dog and the root beer float!

This "Giant Orange" was built in the 1920's to be a roadside juice stand, but since 1947 it's been home to Mark's Hot Dogs.

This vintage hot dog stand is one of the few local restaurants that still offers carhop service.

PUP PARTY

Where can you hang out with thousands of dogs?

Bark in the Park is the largest dog festival in the United States. In 2019, this annual fall event packed more than 15,000 dog lovers and 3,900 dogs into little William Street Park in downtown's Naglee Park neighborhood. People and their pups come to watch dog agility and other sports demonstrations, sheep herding demonstrations, and dog costume contests. More than 75 vendors sell all manner of dog-related gifts, food, and supplies. Animal rescue groups bring out adoptable pets you can add to your pack, and veterinarian offices do discount vaccines and microchipping on-site. Above all, for one day, the neighborhood becomes a giant dog park where (well-behaved and leashed) dogs can enjoy being with other dogs and the people who love them.

The event started in 1996 as a recreational meetup for a small group of neighborhood dog owners. It's grown every year and now attracts people and their dogs from across the Bay Area.

DOG DAY

What: Bark in the Park, an annual gathering of dog lovers and their furry friends.

Where: William Street Park, S. 16th St. and E. William St.

Cost: Free; $6 donation per adult is recommended.

Pro Tip: Proceeds benefit local animal shelters including Humane Society Silicon Valley and the San Jose Animal Care Center.

Prefer to chill with cats? The Dancing Cat (702 E. Julian St.) is a nonprofit animal rescue and cozy "adoption lounge" where you enjoy the company of a dozen free-roaming adoptable cats.

Doting dog owners prepare their pups to compete in a group obedience contest.

This cool canine came wearing shades to protect from the bright September sun.

FIRST IN FLIGHT

What aviation pioneer gave his life flying over the Santa Clara Valley?

One of the early pioneers in flight, John Joseph Montgomery was an inventor and Santa Clara University professor at the turn of the 20th century. Montgomery has been recognized for being the first to invent a heavier-than-air flying machine that could be controlled by the pilot. In his early experiments, he was also the first to use some other aeronautic technologies still used in modern aircraft, including the rear stabilizer and flexible wing tips.

Growing up, Montgomery was always fascinated by flight, watching birds as they moved through the sky. He tinkered with new technology and advances in engineering that promised the future of human aviation. In 1897, he took a job as a professor of physics at Santa Clara University. During his time off, he would travel down to the hilly Evergreen area, where he had permission from a local family to fly on their ranch. The steep hills allowed him to ascend on foot and jump off without having to be lifted by a hot air balloon. He even named one of his glider models "The Evergreen." Over the years, Montgomery would conduct dozens of test flights in this area and others closer to home, even landing gliders on Santa Clara University's campus and in the middle of The Alameda.

In 1911, Montgomery launched his final flight over the Evergreen Hills. On a routine flight, his glider hit a cable, which sent the aircraft crashing to the ground. He died on-site from a gruesome head injury.

Visit the Montgomery Hill Observatory for one of their free monthly public stargazing programs, led by Evergreen Valley College astronomy professors.

You can hike the hills where Montgomery performed his early flying experiments at Montgomery Hill Park.

A sculpture of Montgomery's glider wing stands near the hills where he lost his life.

Some believe that Montgomery's failure to be recognized for his achievements stems from an anti-California bias (the Wright brothers were on the East Coast, which is where the textbooks were written lauding their milestones), but some believe this was driven by Montgomery himself. The inventor was always afraid that his discoveries would be stolen. He usually worked alone and didn't leave many sketches or documentation of his experiments, even though many took place a decade or more before other well-known inventors were experimenting with similar technologies.

GLIDING ALONG

What: A monument to early flight pioneer John J. Montgomery, shaped like a wing of his glider "The Evergreen"

Where: The monument stands on the southeast corner of the intersection of San Felipe Rd. and Yerba Buena Rd.

Cost: Free

Pro Tip: You can hike through the hills where Montgomery flew and, unfortunately, perished at nearby Montgomery Hill Park.

JUST MY TYPE

Where can you learn how books were made 100 years ago?

In San Jose's History Park, there's a tiny museum that will transport book and graphic design lovers back to the days when the layout of every publication was meticulously crafted by an expert tradesperson who set every single word by hand.

Each weekend, docents from the San Jose Printers' Guild, an association of letterpress print enthusiasts, give tours of this print shop, similar to one that might have operated in San Jose at the turn of the twentieth century. These businesses did small projects such as brochures, flyers, business cards, and stationery. Today these volunteers show visitors how to set type by hand and let them print their own keepsake cards or bookmarks using a tabletop press and handset wooden type.

Throughout the year, the guild hosts printmaking workshops and events, including their big annual celebration of all things printed and typed, the San Francisco Bay Area Printers Fair and Wayzgoose. The festival is inspired by the old tradition of

GET STAMPED

What: The Print Shop run by volunteers of the San Jose Printers' Guild

Where: History Park, 635 Phelan Ave.

Cost: Free

Pro Tip: Visit annual SF Bay Area Printer's Fair & Wayzgoose for a celebration of vintage printing, fine paper, and book arts.

The Print Shop is dedicated to preserving and sharing the lost art of designing and printing books, magazines, posters, and newspapers.

A member of the San Jose Printers' Guild demonstrates how to use a manual printing press.

a "wayzgoose," a party thrown by a master printer for his staff to celebrate the end of summer and marking the time of the year when they would have to start working by candlelight. At this event, the San Jose Printers' Guild hosts hands-on letterpress, screen printing, paper making, and bookbinding demonstrations. Vendors sell letterpress printed cards, art books, artisan paper, ink, vintage books, and for those who want to go all in, vintage printing presses.

THE EARLIEST EVS

Where can you take a ride on a 100-year-old electric car?

More than a century before electric cars were common on Bay Area freeways, there were electric-powered streetcars traveling all across the Santa Clara Valley.

From 1880 to 1938, electric trolleys were the main source of transportation. San Jose had the first electric streetcar system west of the Rockies, and the region had 126 miles of track connecting all corners of the valley and offering connections to San Francisco and beyond via the Southern Pacific Railroad.

Every spring, a seasonal Blossom Trolley ran a 65-mile day trip across the Santa Clara Valley, letting riders view apricot, peach, and pear blossoms in orchards across the valley floor, all for just 35 cents.

If you want to take a ride on one of those first "electric vehicles," stop by History Park each weekend for a free ride. The Trolley Barn was built in 1984 in the style of trolley buildings from the early part of the

TROLLEY TIME

What: The Trolley Barn

Where: History Park, 635 Phelan Ave.

Cost: Free

Pro Tip: The park offers free vintage trolley rides on most Saturday and Sunday afternoons, but rain cancels.

At the turn of the 20th century, thousands of people from downtown San Jose would hop on an electric streetcar each weekend and ride it to Alum Rock Park to spend the day at the hot spring spas.

Take a ride on a vintage electric streetcar and learn more about historic transit technology at the Trolly Barn in History Park.

20th century. Volunteers and members of the California Trolley & Railroad Corporation have restored a number of antique trolleys and streetcars and display them in the barn. Every Saturday and Sunday afternoon they offer free rides across the park. On a recent visit, I got to ride in a lovely 1930s trolley that had originally been used in the City of Fresno. Before it was carefully restored, the previous owner had used it as a chicken coop in their backyard!

SPRINGS ETERNAL

What popular park used to be a famous health resort?

One of my favorite things to do in San Jose is take a hike at one of our many parks and open space preserves. The oldest and largest park in the city is Alum Rock Park, though today's wild hiking trails and undisturbed access to nature are very different draws from what it offered a hundred years ago.

SOAK IN THIS

What: The old stone grottoes at Alum Rock Park

Where: 15350 Penitencia Creek Rd.

Cost: $6 to park at the Alum Rock Visitor Center & Youth Science Institute parking lots.

Pro Tip: Parking is free in the Eagle Rock & Rustic Lands parking lots.

Alum Rock Park was designated as a public park by the California State Legislature in 1872 and credited as being the first city park in California. For just 25 cents, you could hop on a steam train and later an electric streetcar in downtown San Jose and take it all the way into the park, where as many as 10,000 visitors would gather on a single Sunday afternoon.

The biggest draw was the famous mineral springs. People would travel from around the country to soak in various hot and cold pools of mineral water that 19th century doctors claimed were good for various ailments.

From 1891 on, the city built a bandstand, a restaurant, ornate stone grottoes, bathhouses, and a large indoor swimming pool with a two-story slide, called the "Natatorium."

Because of the heavy visitor traffic and development, by the 1970s, the native plants and wildlife population had declined. The city decided to return the park to a more natural state, removing the swimming pool, many of the buildings,

You can hike along the ruins of old hot spring grottoes at Alum Rock Park.

and closing off some areas. As the natural habitat recovered, many species of native wildlife and plants returned, and the park is now a popular destination for school groups. The environmental education nonprofit Youth Science Institute is based on-site, organizing programs that teach kids about nature.

Today, you can see the ruins of the old stone grottoes and smell the sulfur spring along the Penitencia Creek and Mineral Springs Loop trails. The park facilities building now stands on the site of the Natatorium, and the adjacent public restrooms were once part of the original pool house.

Alum Rock Park once had a 2,000-ton black rock that they claimed to be one of the largest meteorites in the world. It was a major tourist destination in the park. Because of its high manganese content, during World War I it was sold for smelting as part of the war effort.

ANCIENT GIANTS

How did pioneering environmental activists fight to save California's redwood forests?

"Imagine a time when the whole peninsula from San Francisco to San Jose shall become one great city," starts the quote. (You don't actually have to try hard to imagine this.) "Then picture, at its very doorstep, this magnificent domain of redwood forests and running streams, the breathing place of millions of cramped and crowded denizens of the city."

These were the prescient words of local environmental activist Carrie Stevens Walter in 1901. Walter was a poet and educator and member of the San Jose Woman's Club. She was horrified to see loggers clear the ancient redwood forests in the Santa Cruz Mountains in the late 19th century, leaving bare hills. She joined a group of other concerned neighbors led by acclaimed painter and photographer Andrew P. Hill to protect the remaining old-growth coast redwoods.

Thanks to their persistent lobbying efforts, the state legislature passed a bill in 1901 that officially designated Big Basin Redwoods as California's first state park. Today, you can stand in awe of Big Basin's ancient and massive trees, some as old as 1,800 years and as tall as the Statue of Liberty. The park offers visitors 80 miles of hiking trails, hidden waterfalls, and stunning views of the Pacific Ocean.

As one of the "millions of cramped and crowded denizens of the city" that Walter imagined, I'm grateful for their work.

You can see the home where environmentalist Andrew P. Hill lived from 1898 to his death in 1922 in San Jose's History Park. It was originally located at 1350 Sherman St.

A grove of ancient coast redwood trees at Big Basin State Park.

REDWOODS & WATERFALLS

What: Big Basin Redwoods State Park

Where: 21600 Big Basin Way, Boulder Creek

Cost: $10 day use fee, per vehicle

Pro Tip: Visit in the winter or spring to see waterfalls.

I'M WITH THE BAND

How do we know what migratory birds pass through the Santa Clara Valley?

For almost 40 years, the nonprofit San Francisco Bay Bird Observatory (SFBBO) has studied the local bird populations that live along the San Francisco Bay. The organization collects information that helps us understand how these populations are changing over time.

"Climate change is affecting a lot of bird species," says San Francisco Bay Bird Observatory Landbirds Program Manager, Josh Scullen. "If you don't have baseline data to understand the normal population variation, you won't know when to panic. We are out there on the front lines of defense, working to spot these changes."

The organization's Coyote Creek Field Station is hidden on a private water district-owned road near where McCarthy Blvd. crosses Highway 237 in Milpitas. Coyote Creek is the last natural stream system remaining in the Santa Clara Valley, and it provides vital habitat for birds and other wildlife. On this creekside site, researchers capture passing birds—from tiny hummingbirds to larger raptors, such as hawks. Using a sequence of nearly invisible hanging nets to capture the bird temporarily, researchers gently extract the animals so that they can take a variety of measurements to understand their

A few times a year the organization opens up the private field center and invites members of the public to watch this delicate process and learn about the efforts to protect native bird populations in the Bay and across the Pacific Flyway.

A staff member of the San Francisco Bay Bird Observatory gently extracts a warbling vireo from a net at the Coyote Creek Field Station.

age, reproductive patterns, and health. Before releasing the birds, they attach a tiny and lightweight numbered band to one leg and log them in an international database so that they can be identified anywhere in the world. The process is quick, and the skilled researchers are careful not to harm the birds.

The changes they've seen have been mixed. Some species have declined, such as the warbling vireo, a small, yellow bird that used to be very common and now is spotted only a few times a year. Others, such as the song sparrow, had previously been in decline, but the population is showing growth after a few decades of successful habitat restoration work along Coyote Creek.

BIRD'S-EYE VIEW

What: San Francisco Bay Bird Observatory's Coyote Creek Field Station in Milpitas

Where: Access to this private research facility is by appointment only.

Cost: Varies

Pro Tip: Public tours are held seasonally from April 15 to October 15. You can sign up for the SFBBO's email list to be notified when they are scheduled.

WAVE OF THE FUTURE

Where will our water come from?

We recycle everything—paper, plastic, metals, and if you compost, even food. Why not recycle our sewage and turn it back into water that we can drink? Actually, we already do!

The Silicon Valley Advanced Water Purification Center on Zanker Road in North San Jose produces eight million gallons of recycled water a day and is the largest water purification plant in Northern California. Since 2014, the facility, managed by Valley Water and supported by the cities of San Jose and Santa Clara, has taken lightly treated urban sewage and turned it into clear, safe water that meets California's drinking water quality standards. Until now, the recycled water that has gone through a multistep cleansing and disinfection process using microfiltration, reverse osmosis, and ultraviolet light, has been used for non-potable uses, such as watering landscaping and flushing toilets at large facilities, such as Levi Stadium and Mineta San Jose International Airport.

In the next few months, the plant will add an additional treatment step called Advanced Oxidation, which adds a bit of natural hydrogen peroxide to the end product to dissolve anything else that wasn't already destroyed. This step will make the end product even cleaner than state standards and make it possible to serve the water directly to the public to drink.

Currently, 7 percent of the water used in the South Bay is recycled, and Valley Water is trying to surpass 10 percent in the next few years. By 2028, the agency hopes these recycling projects will meet the water needs of 370,000 people.

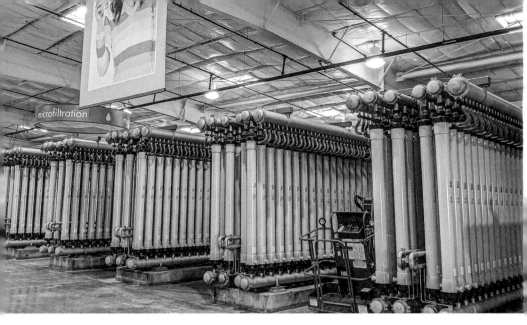

The Silicon Valley Advanced Water Purification Center, turns lightly treated urban sewage into safe, clean drinking water.

While the water is perfectly safe at this point, due to public perception and the "yuck factor," the agency plans to inject the recycled water back into the groundwater system, so it will still be a few steps removed from the tap. A similar process has been in place in Orange County, California, where they have been adding recycled water back into reservoirs since 2008.

Why recycle wastewater? The more recycled water we use, the less we have to extract from our limited groundwater, rivers, and streams. It also provides a reliable and drought-proof source of water, especially important in our changing climate.

Wastewater recycling is also more energy efficient and has fewer negative environmental impacts than technologies like desalination.

FUTURE-PROOFED

What: Silicon Valley Advanced Water Purification Center

Where: 4190 Zanker Rd.

Cost: Free

Pro Tip: You can sign up for a free tour of the Advanced Water Purification Center on their website: www.purewater4u.org

DROWNED TOWN

Where was there once a town on stilts hovering over the San Francisco Bay?

If you are riding the Amtrak train from San Jose to Oakland, you might notice some old buildings sinking into the salt marsh along the Bay just south of Fremont. These structures are the last remaining signs of the ghost town, Drawbridge.

For almost a hundred years, the town was a weekend getaway destination for duck hunters, fishermen, and sun-seeking San Franciscans. At its peak, the town had 90 hotels, cabins, and saloons all perched on stilts to raise them out of the marshy ground. On some weekends, the small community had as many as 600 guests. The town was known to be relatively lawless without a police or county sheriff presence, and prostitution, gambling, and alcohol were easy to come by even during Prohibition.

By the 20th century, Drawbridge had started to decline, mostly because hunters had decimated the local waterfowl population. The Bay became increasingly polluted with raw sewage, and the fish population declined. The town was also sinking quickly due to groundwater pumping for valley agriculture. The last residents moved out in 1976.

SINKING STOP

What: The ghost town of Drawbridge

Where: In the marshlands on the southeast side of the San Francisco Bay. This land is currently protected as part of the Don Edwards San Francisco Bay National Wildlife Refuge.

Cost: Cost of an Amtrak or ACE train ticket

Pro Tip: Public access is not allowed, and trespassing is illegal on this piece of federal wildlife habitat. The only way to see the last remaining structures is to take any Amtrak or Altamont Corridor Express (ACE) train from San Jose or Santa Clara to points north.

164

Only a few crumbling buildings remain of the bayside ghost town, Drawbridge.

By this point, many of the structures were already badly decomposed, and deemed not worth restoring. The remaining salt marsh in the area also became recognized as essential habitat. For some endangered wildlife species, such as the salt harvest mouse and a bird called the Ridgeway's rail, efforts were made to let this area return to nature. Today, there is no public access allowed on this highly fragile salt marsh area. As conservationists have restored other baylands, the populations of these threatened species have started to rebound.

As climate change causes bay waters to rise, those last signs of Drawbridge will disappear, so hop on a train and spot them while you can.

Today, the Don Edwards Refuge to the north and Alviso Marina County Park to the south are world-famous birding and wildlife-watching spots.

LOSING GROUND

What threatened wildlife live among us?

What do you think of when you think of an endangered species? Elephants, rhinos, or tigers, maybe?

When thinking of these iconic animals, it can be easy to forget that our planet is changing locally, too, and endangered and threatened species are all around us. Over the last 200 years, the Bay Area has lost 90 percent of its historic tidal marshlands, and human activity and urban development have damaged much of the native habitat.

Some of the most threatened species in the Santa Clara Valley include the palm-size western burrowing owl, which makes its home exclusively in ground squirrel holes. The development of large open fields across the valley floor has caused the population to plummet. In the 1980s, local researchers counted more than 500 burrowing owls in 250 breeding locations across the county. Today, there are fewer than 48 owls remaining and only four breeding locations.

The Bay checkerspot butterfly relies on a very specific plant host that only lives on a very specific type of soil. Once found all over the Bay Area, the checkerspot can now be found only in a handful of places, including Coyote Ridge Open Space Preserve.

The California tiger salamander, California red-legged frog, and western pond turtles all live in the Santa Clara Valley's native streams and wetlands, which are fewer and farther between. Other larger local species, such as the mountain lion

The Santa Clara Valley Habitat Agency manages a 50-year regional plan guiding local efforts to protect 18 threatened species and native habitat.

While the western burrowing owl was once common across Santa Clara County, today fewer than 48 birds remain. Photo courtesy of Eileen Johnson

and tule elk, are both suffering population declines and genetic conditions caused by habitat fragmentation and inbreeding.

Active habitat restoration projects are present all over the county, and most really need volunteers, so if you want to help save our local threatened species, contact the organizations that are doing this work.

WONDERFUL WILDLIFE

What: Bay checkerspot butterflies, western burrowing owl, California red-legged frog, California tiger salamander, western pond turtle, tricolored blackbird, and the San Joaquin kit fox are a few of the threatened species that make their home in and around San Jose.

Where: Various locations

Cost: Free

Pro Tip: The Santa Clara Valley Audubon Society, San Francisco Bay Bird Observatory, Santa Clara Valley Open Space Authority, and Midpeninsula Regional Open Space District are always looking for volunteers to help remove invasive plants and maintain suitable habitat for threatened wildlife. The Wildlife Center of Silicon Valley is always seeking volunteers to help care for sick and injured native wildlife at their rehabilitation center.

LOST LAKES

Where can you see a disappearing lake?

Before European settlers started to arrive in the 18th and 19th centuries, the Santa Clara Valley looked very different. Wetlands stretched from the Bay up and around the creeks and through the Santa Clara Valley. Some of these wetlands only flooded seasonally and provided important habitat for native and migratory birds and other wildlife.

Unfortunately, over the next 250 years, early residents drained more than 90 percent of that land and diverted streams into concrete channels to make the area easier to develop.

The largest remaining seasonal lake, an area called Laguna Seca (which aptly means "dry lagoon"), once covered more than 1,000 acres south of San Jose in the Coyote Valley. In the past, the lake was filled almost year-round. Today, the water level is lower and disappears earlier in the dry season.

LIQUID LANE

What: The Bay Area's largest remaining seasonal wetland, Laguna Seca, is part of the permanently protected North Coyote Valley Conservation Area.

Where: In the winter and spring, watch for this seasonal lagoon on the west side of Santa Teresa Blvd. about 1.5 miles north of Bailey Ave.

Cost: Free

Pro Tip: The Santa Clara Valley Open Space Authority manages this protected land and hosts free nature walks to learn about this important habitat.

Laguna Seca is a great spot for birdwatching. Some of the species you can see here are the yellow-billed magpie, white-tailed kite, and the brightly colored western meadowlark.

This seasonal wetland once covered more than a thousand acres across the Coyote Valley South of San Jose. Photo courtesy of Santa Clara Valley Open Space Authority

Even as it disappears, this unique habitat has many benefits for our community. Beyond providing wildlife habitat, wetlands, such as Laguna Seca, help prevent San Jose from flooding in winter storms by slowing rainwater and keeping it from flowing into overloaded creeks and streams. Wetlands also help capture atmospheric carbon, providing a buffer against climate change.

The Laguna Seca region was permanently protected in a recent $93.5 million deal between the City of San Jose and local land conservation organizations. You can visit the protected landscape, now called the North Coyote Valley Conservation Area, on guided hikes hosted by the Santa Clara Valley Open Space Authority.

A HEAVENLY SITE

Where can you see from Monterey Bay to the Sierras?

One of the best vistas over the Santa Clara Valley has a long and winding history. Mount Umunhum was traditionally a spiritual center for the Amah Mutsun indigenous community. Later, the land was occupied by the US government and used as an Air Force base and Cold War–era radar tower. Today, it's managed by the Midpeninsula Open Space District, and it's part of the 18,000-acre Sierra Azul Open Space Preserve in the hills east of Los Gatos.

The name, derived from the local native language, means "resting place of the hummingbird," and migratory hummingbirds do come up to the peak. "Mt. Um" is one of the four highest peaks in the Bay Area along with Mount Hamilton, Mount Diablo, and Mount Tamalpais. On a clear day at the summit, you can see from the Monterey Peninsula over to the Sierra Nevada. The hiking trails are part of the Bay Area Ridge Trail, an attempt to connect the ridges around all 10 Bay Area counties into one continuous 550-mile park.

During the Cold War, Air Force watchmen would scan the skies in search of Russian bombers. The Almaden Air Force Station had residences for officers and families living on-site, including a swimming pool and two-lane bowling alley. When

WHAT A VIEW

What: Mount Umunhum, one of the highest peaks in the Santa Cruz Mountains

Where: Sierra Azul Open Space Preserve, Mt. Umunhum Rd.

Cost: Free

Pro Tip: Take your choice of driving to the summit parking lot or hiking up from the Bald Mountain (3.5 miles, one way) or Jacques Ridge (9 miles, one way) parking areas. Take your time on the drive. Roads are narrow, windy, and steep. Use low gear on the way down.

The view from Mount Umunhum, one of the Bay Area's tallest peaks. On a clear day at the summit, you can see from the Monterey Bay to the Sierra Nevada.

satellites made this manual scanning obsolete, the Air Force decommissioned the base. The Midpeninsula Open Space district later acquired it and worked with the government to do cleanup and restoration. While they demolished most of the original buildings, they maintained the 85-foot-tall tower, which stands like a beacon over the Santa Clara Valley. At time of print, the agency is working to shore up the crumbling landmark tower and keep visitors safe.

This mountain peak is again accessible to the local indigenous community. As part of the restoration effort, the district worked with the Amah Mutsun Tribal Band to design a ceremonial circle where they can once again dance and engage with this sacred space. Members of the community hadn't had this opportunity for more than a hundred years.

On the way up to Mount Umunhum, you'll drive on forested Hicks Road, which local legend says is either haunted or the site of local troublemakers who will try to run you off the road.

HICKS ROAD

Why do people avoid driving here after dark?

There's one South Bay destination that comes up more than almost any other when you ask longtime locals about unusual places. "Haunted" Hicks Road stretches from the edge of San Jose's urban sprawl at Camden Avenue through 10 miles of total wilderness to Almaden Reservoir. During the day, it's a lovely drive along a winding creek, but after dark, legends say that spooky things start to happen.

These legends date back to the 1970s and have been passed from person to person over the years. Many of the myths involve an organized colony, like a religious community or cult, or family that is actively trying to keep people out. Stories range from the otherworldly tales of ghosts, UFOs, and a reclusive family afflicted with albinism to the more believable but seedy stories of satanic rituals, cult leaders, and criminal behavior, such as cars trying to run them off the road.

While some of the stories probably have their origin in youthful imagination at slumber parties, others are likely rooted in truth. Whether they are a product of the stories

HAUNTED OR NOT

What: A mythic local road

Where: Hicks Road

Cost: Free

Pro Tip: Avoid at night (obviously!)

Almost everyone seems to have a creepy or unusual story about this rural road.

Hicks Road is a winding, rural road that locals claim to be haunted.

or a cause of the stories, the rural road tends to draw people looking to play pranks, get away from society, and consume various substances.

Because of the local lore, the city has always had a problem with people stealing Hicks Road signs. I wouldn't recommend it. From what I hear, Hicks Road is not a place where you want to get lost.

PARANORMAL PROWL

Where can you go to hear a good ghost story?

With so much history in San Jose, it's no surprise that there are a lot of spooky legends and haunted tales. One way to learn about these stories is to join the Bay Area Ghost Hunters, a local meetup group for people interested in the paranormal.

I WANT TO BELIEVE

What: The Bay Area Ghost Hunters, a public meetup group for anyone interested in paranormal research and investigation.

Where: Various locations

Cost: Some meetups at restaurants and bars are free, and you are expected to order your own food/drinks. Group leaders charge a modest admission fee for organized tours, group meals, and ticketed events.

Pro Tip: Join the group to learn about future events: www.meetup.com/Bay-Area-Ghost-Hunters

The organization is led by Adrienne Foster, a lifelong San Jose resident, writer, and paranormal enthusiast. Foster knows all the local haunted places and organizes ghost and history walks at sites around Silicon Valley. On a recent downtown walk, she pointed out places like San Jose State's old gymnasium, which was a processing area for Japanese internees during WWII. Staff and students say they can sometimes hear unexplained voices and crying late at night.

Anyone who is curious about the haunted and paranormal are invited to join their events. According to their Meetup.com profile, "Skepticism is appreciated, but close-mindedness is not."

History isn't just about facts and numbers, it's about people and the stories of their lives. Ghost hunters try to empathize with those who suffered great tragedy and feel the pain they felt while they were living. The public tours draw a mix of avid ghost hunters, curious newcomers, psychic mediums, and other "sensitive" types who are able to detect paranormal activity.

Hayes Mansion, now a hotel in the Edenvale neighborhood, was built by Mary Hayes Cheynoweth, a spiritual healer known to have conducted seances in the house. The hotel is said to be haunted.

On the balcony at GrandView Restaurant.

One favorite local "haunt" is GrandView Restaurant (15005 Mt Hamilton Rd.). Both diners and staff report oddly flickering lights and seeing a girl looking out over the balcony who disappears if you try to approach her.

DONNER DESTINY

Where did survivors of the legendary Donner Party wind up?

From a very young age, every California student learns the tragic pioneer story of the Donner Party, a group of midwestern migrants who journeyed across the country in a wagon train to build a new life on the West Coast. In the winter of 1846, the team's leaders made a series of mistakes and wound up stranded in the Sierra Nevada mountains during a snowstorm. Almost half of the party died from hypothermia, and those that remained faced a terrible choice and resorted to cannibalism to survive.

After finally being rescued, 13 survivors eventually settled in San Jose, including Eliza Poor Donner, Mary Donner, James and Margaret Reed, and the Reed children.

In 1849, James Reed became the San Jose Chief of Police, and during California's constitutional convention, he led the campaign to make San Jose the state's first capital.

Eliza Poor Donner later shared her firsthand account of the journey in a 1911 book *Expedition of the Donner Party and Its Tragic Fate*. She married San Jose business leader Sherman Otis Houghton and commissioned a local architect to build them a large home downtown. Over the city's history, the house was

STARTING OVER

What: Site of a home owned by Eliza Donner, a survivor of the ill-fated Donner Party. The house burned down in 2007, and an affordable rental community was built on-site, named in tribute to this history.

Where: Donner Lofts, 158 E. St. John St.

Cost: Free to view, private residence. Do not disturb residents.

Pro Tip: You can see the graves of several members of the Donner and Reed families at Oak Hill Memorial Park.

The Donner Lofts on the site of Eliza Poor Donner and husband Sherman Otis Houghton's home.

moved twice, ending up at the corner of 4th and St. John Streets, where it was placed on the National Register of Historic Places in 2002. Though the Donner-Houghton house burned down in 2007, it was replaced by the Donner Lofts, a much-needed affordable housing community.

Young Illinois lawyer Abraham Lincoln was a friend and army bunkmate of James Reed and almost joined the Donner Party on this fateful trip. His wife, Mary Todd Lincoln, was pregnant at the time and didn't want to risk going West, so they decided to stay in Illinois. She went to the Donner Party's departure in Springfield to wave them all goodbye.

THE FEARLESS GEERS

What local family toured the world, performing high-wire stunts on bikes?

Three generations of a world-famous acrobatic family got their start practicing unusual stunts in the backyard of their Willow Glen home.

In the late 1800s, Albert Geer started a vaudeville troupe he called "Frances Dainty & Company." The Dainty company specialized in bicycle stunts, balancing unusual things on a bike, jump roping on a unicycle, and crossing a high wire on a bike.

The company traveled all around the United States, Europe, and Asia performing these curious acts. Albert's son, Cyril, performed along with him and took over the troop after his father's death in 1922. Cyril's son, Francis, was born on tour and also later performed with his dad and mom.

The Geer family lived in the same Victorian home on Coe Avenue in Willow Glen's Palm Haven neighborhood from 1886 to 1999. When they finally sold the home, the family donated paraphernalia to History San Jose, including costumes, home videos, and the Tagalog and Chinese language flyers from their performances in Asia.

HIGH WIRED

What: A Victorian house where three generations of the Geer family lived and practiced death-defying stunts that they performed around the world as part of their touring act, the Frances Dainty Vaudeville Company

Where: 795 Coe Ave.

Cost: Free to view, private residence. Do not disturb.

Pro Tip: You can view an old home video of one of the Dainty's backyard practice sessions either on History San Jose's YouTube channel or by searching the video site for "Frances Dainty."

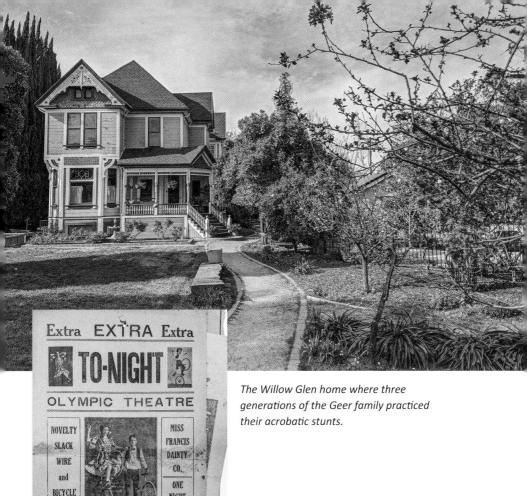

Extra EXTRA Extra

TO-NIGHT

OLYMPIC THEATRE

NOVELTY
SLACK
WIRE
and
BICYCLE
ARTISTS

MISS
FRANCIS
DAINTY
CO.

ONE
NIGHT
ONLY

Special For One Night Only From the Grand Theatre at North Yakima

Miss Francis Dainty & Co., has been one of the feature acts with Ringling Bros. circus for the past season. They sail on March 9th on the steamer Sierra to do an engagement in Honolulu, and go from there to China and Japan continueing on to Australia and New Zeland.

HERE ONE NIGHT ONLY   General Admission 15 Cents

The Willow Glen home where three generations of the Geer family practiced their acrobatic stunts.

From the late 19th to mid-20th century, "Frances Dainty & Company" was a local vaudeville performing group that toured the world.

One advertisement billed them as, "The World's Greatest Cyclists in Extraordinary Feats of Cycling Riding and Balancing. Whirling, twirling, twisting, turning, circling cyclists in a whirlwind of thrills, quicker than shots fired from a rapid fire gun."

TRYIN' TO BE GOOD

What's so rotten about these convenience stores?

If you have ever stopped to fill up your tank and wondered about the origins of the oddly named local gas station, Rotten Robbie, and their even stranger tagline, here's the story.

Before World War II, local businessman Herb Richards started an oil company in San Jose called Coast Oil. At the time, all gas stations were full-service, and drivers were not allowed to pump their own gas. Richards led a campaign to support self-service stations, arguing it would allow companies to sell gas at a lower price. When the bill was eventually passed, Richards opened the first self-service gas station in Northern California in 1948.

After merging with another San Jose–based company, Robinson's Oil, in 1971, Richards along with Robinson's founder, Dan Robinson, started buying up other local gas stations. They wanted a unique and memorable name for the newly consolidated brand. Herb's wife's name was Nell, so he threw out the idea of "Nasty Nell" that he quickly rejected, knowing she would not appreciate it. He then suggested "Rotten Robbie," inspired by his partner, and Dan agreed.

The company consistently offered the lowest prices around. They also offered interesting promotions, such as monthly giveaways of a Cadillac, and a loyalty stamp program that frequent customers could redeem for discounts and free goods. Low prices paired with promos like these helped people get over the hurdle of buying from a "rotten" company. In 2014, a rebranding campaign put the store's new (and self-deprecating) tagline, "Tryin' to be good" out in the community on signs and staff name tags. Company President and CEO Tom Robinson said in a 2016 interview, "I believe companies make a mistake when they say, 'we're perfect.' That's hard to live up to. We are Rotten Robbie, so we have a bit to overcome anyway."

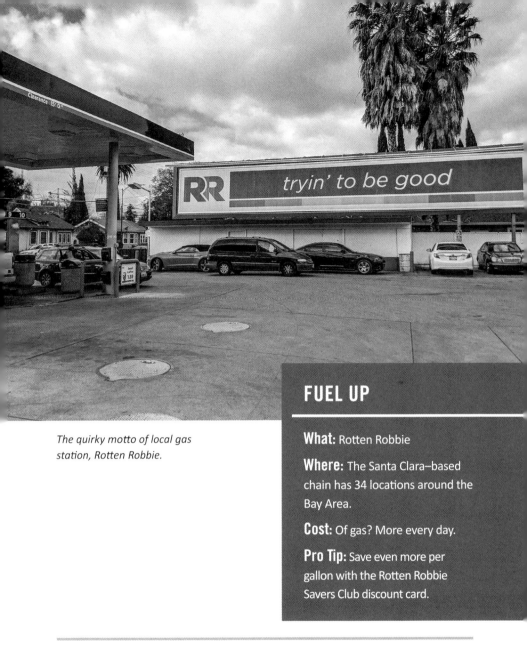

The quirky motto of local gas station, Rotten Robbie.

FUEL UP

What: Rotten Robbie

Where: The Santa Clara–based chain has 34 locations around the Bay Area.

Cost: Of gas? More every day.

Pro Tip: Save even more per gallon with the Rotten Robbie Savers Club discount card.

While you are waiting by the pump, you can thank (or curse) Rotten Robbie founder Herb Richards for campaigning to pass the legislation that allows California drivers to pump their own gas.

CALIFORNIA MODERN

What mid-century architect brought attractive and affordable homes to the masses?

While we're hardly Palm Springs, San Jose has several tracts of stunning mid-century modern homes. These houses were designed by Joseph Eichler, one of the most influential builders of the time. In the 1950s and 1960s, Eichler built more than 11,000 homes in California. In 2019, one of the best preserved tracts of Eichler homes, the Fairglen Additions neighborhood near Willow Glen, was added to the National Register of Historic Places.

These homes, characteristic of the California Modern style, feature flat and low sloped A-frame roofs, floor-to-ceiling windows, and open floor plans.

Growing up, Eichler's family had lived for a time in a Frank Lloyd Wright–designed home in Hillsborough. This experience inspired his love of modern design and his desire to make good design affordable for ordinary families.

In the 1950s and 1960s, the Santa Clara Valley was growing quickly with the rise of booming postwar technology, defense, and manufacturing industries raising the demand for affordable, middle-class housing.

Eichler's firm had a nondiscrimination policy at a time when many suburban home builders refused to sell homes to Black and minority families, claiming more inclusive sales would reduce property values. In 1958, Eichler resigned from the Associated Home Builders of San Francisco, due to their support for these discriminatory practices.

One of the many well-preserved Eichler homes in the Fairglen Additions neighborhood of Willow Glen.

Eichler's designs were truly made for California, integrating the indoors and the outdoors with open, airy rooms, floor to ceiling windows, skylights, and outdoor patios and living spaces. The neighborhoods were designed to connect the individual residences with local parks and community centers.

MOD SQUAD

What: Several of Joseph Eichler's residential subdivisions are located in the Bay Area, including a few in San Jose.

Where: The largest tract of Eichler homes in San Jose is the Fairglen Additions neighborhood near the intersection of Fairglen Ave. and Fairwood Ave.

Cost: Free

Pro Tip: All homes are privately owned; do not disturb the residents.

STITCHED TOGETHER

Where can you see textiles and clothing as art?

If you're picturing a fussy floral and patchwork blanket on the back of your grandma's sofa when you think of quilts, San Jose's Museum of Quilts and Textiles might surprise you.

The first of its kind in the United States when it opened in 1977, the museum was started by a local quilt association to display historic and family quilts that they didn't want to just store in their closets. Over the years, the collection expanded to include displays featuring a mix of historic and contemporary fabric arts and works that play with different materials and technology.

"People who come here for the first time are always surprised by what they see, and most of our regular visitors continue to be surprised by what we are exhibiting," says Nancy Bavor, the museum's executive director.

CUTTING EDGE

What: San Jose Museum of Quilts & Textiles

Where: 520 S. First Ave.

Cost: $6.50–$8

Pro Tip: On the first Friday of the month, pay what you can during the day and get free admission from 7:00 to 10:00 p.m.

In some recent exhibits, the museum displayed hand-woven Mayan textiles from Guatemala, an examination of the role embroidered head coverings play in the identity of women in the

The museum works to honor the under-recognized and often home-based labor of women both as art and as a critical means of sharing stories and culture.

184

Find a surprising array of clothing and textile art at the San Jose Museum of Quilts and Textiles.

Punjab region of India, and artists who look at the role of clothing in our lives through photography, sculpture, and other mediums.

The museum doesn't shy away from exhibits that prompt discussion about the most challenging and important social issues of our day. The recent exhibit "Guns: Loaded Conversations" shared a mix of textile works inspired by gun violence in America, including quilts made by a group of Chicago teens representing how gun violence has affected their lives, and a cross stitch depiction of the 1999 massacre at Columbine High School.

GET LIT

Where can you see a dancing pig in downtown San Jose?

The 1950s and 1960s were the golden age of the automobile in San Jose. As the city grew outward, businesses would compete for traffic by creating colorful neon signs and eye-catching displays that you would see driving by. An always shrinking number of those curious signs remain, but one local favorite just got a facelift.

If you go to a Sharks game at night, you're sure to see the bow-tied dancing pig just a few blocks from the SAP Center. The animated little piggie sign dates back to the 1950s when there was a local meat processing plant called Stephen's Meat Products on the site. Though the plant is no more, the brand lives on under ownership of local meat producer Bassian Farms. They still produce sausages under the Stephen's brand using their original recipes.

RETRO GLOW

What: This posh pig marks the site of the former Stephen's Meat Products company. If you see the sign at night, the pig appears to dance.

Where: 105 S. Montgomery St.

Cost: Free

Pro Tip: Pick up a copy of *The San Jose Signs Project: A Guide to the Vintage Signage of San Jose*, published by Preservation Action Council of San Jose. This guide shares more than two dozen classic signs and statues in San Jose.

The Stephen's Meat neon sign was recently restored, letting the piggie dance again after a fund-raising campaign by local historic advocacy group, Preservation Action Council of San Jose. The organization has also made a push to protect other neon signs from the era.

Babe the Muffler Man is one of 225 giant muffler men that once stood in the United States.

Beyond the neon, a number of other historic figurative signs and roadside kitsch dot the urban landscape. These include Babe the Muffler Man (808 The Alameda), one of 225 giant muffler men that once stood in the United States, the Cambrian Park Plaza's spinning carousel sign (14900 Camden Ave.), and the last original Kentucky Fried Chicken bucket sign (250 N. Bascom Ave.) still standing in the US.

SOURCES

A Mammoth Discovery
Visit to the site; https://www.cdm.org/mammothdiscovery/index.html; https://www.
mercurynews.com/2008/09/24/lupe-the-baby-mammoth-comes-home-to-san-
jose; https://www.sanjoseca.gov/your-government/departments/parks-recreation-
neighborhood-services/outdoor-activities/trail-network/tourism

On the Trail
Guided hike with Les Krammer, docent for the Santa Clara Valley Open Space Authority,
January 2020; https://www.nps.gov/juba/index.htm

A Thousand Drinks
Site visit; *A Self-Governing Dominion, California, 1849-1860* by William Henry Ellison; *Santa
Clara County: Harvest of Change* by Stephen M. Payne; https://www.library.ca.gov/
california-history/previous-ca-capitals

Towering Tomb
Interview with Paul Lynam, Staff Astronomer, UCO/Lick Observatory, October 2019;
https://www.ucolick.org/main/science/telescopes/refractor.html; http://collections.
ucolick.org/archives_on_line/James_Lick.html; https://www.mercurynews.
com/2017/06/12/james-lick-an-eccentrics-legacy; CPI Inflation Calculator: https://www.
officialdata.org/us/inflation/1877?amount=700000

Secrets in the Stacks
Guided tour, October 2019; https://www.sjlibrary.org/recolecciones-king-library-public-art-
collections

Tickled Ivories
Site visit; http://www.orchestriapalmcourt.com/; https://www.kqed.org/
bayareabites/135303/eat-drink-like-youre-in-the-1920s-two-nights-a-week

Enlightening Eats
https://www.chuaducvien.com/; https://www.kqed.org/bayareabites/637/sharing-the-
sacred-community-meals-at-buddhist-and-sikh-temples

Of Unknown Origin
"The Real, True Story of the Mystery of the East Bay Walls" Bay Curious video: https://
youtu.be/OMISe8MKVC4; https://www.kqed.org/news/11689504/uncovering-the-real-
story-behind-the-mysterious-east-bay-walls; "Rock Walls of Mission Peak Regional Park:
An Overview," Courtney Norris & Terryn Buxton for the East Bay Regional Park District,
August 17, 1995.

A Moo with a View
Interviews with Derek Neumann, Santa Clara Valley Open Space Authority, and Clayton
Koopman, cattle rancher and rangeland ecologist; http://news.openspaceauthority.org/
blog/a-grazing-management-strategy-is-key-to-promoting-native-biodiversity; https://
www.sccgov.org/sites/dpd/DocsForms/Documents/SCV_ActionPlan.pdf

Rest in Pieces
Site visit; https://www.mercurynews.com/2009/11/03/new-almaden-cemetery-traces-
ghastly-history; https://www.atlasobscura.com/places/grave-of-bert-barretts-left-arm

Crisis Averted

https://ch.ucpress.edu/content/ucpch/15/1/2.full.pdf; *Bullion Bend: Confederate Stagecoach Robbers, Murder Trials, and the California Supreme Court — Oh My!* by William E. Cole; http://www.sbcwrt.org/sbwp/wp-content/uploads/2013/01/Lincoln-Writ.pdf; *African Americans of San Jose and Santa Clara County* by Jan Batiste Adkins

Monument to Nowhere

https://www.mercurynews.com/2016/01/08/san-joses-infamous-monument-to-nowhere-freeway-interchange-finally-named-after-joe-colla

Sí, Se Puede

America's Social Arsonist Fred Ross and Grassroots Organizing in the Twentieth Century by Gabriel Thompson; https://www.bizjournals.com/sanjose/news/2017/01/11/nations-newest-historic-landmark-honors-san-jose.html; https://chavezfamilyvision.org/about-us

The People's Theater

Zoot Suit and Other Plays, by Luis Valdez; KTEH This is Us profile of Luis Valdez: https://youtu.be/isPFm9A_xRM; "Changing the Narrative: Teatro Visión" Gillian Claus, *Content Magazine*, Jan/Feb 2020

Mountain Charlie

Visit to the site; *Ghost Towns of the Santa Cruz Mountains* by John V. Young; https://www.findagrave.com/memorial/7617864/charles-henry-mckiernan; http://www.mountaincharlie1850.org/mountain_charlie_story.html

Holy Rollers

Holy City Riker's Religious Roadside Attraction by Betty Lewis; Ghost Towns of the Santa Cruz Mountains by John V. Young; https://www.sfchronicle.com/bayarea/article/holy-city-santa-cruz-father-william-riker-13035533.php

Pedal to Poultry

Interview with Scott Vanderlip, February 2020; https://tourdecoop.org

Egg-cellent

Site visit; https://www.cnn.com/travel/article/how-to-eat-balut/index.html

Mane Attraction

https://www.classicfm.com/composers/beethoven/news/lock-hair-auctioned-sothebys/, https://www.sjsu.edu/beethoven/collections_exhibit/beethoven_hair, *Beethoven's Hair: An Extraordinary Historical Odyssey and a Scientific Mystery Solved* by Russell Martin

Furry Friends

Site visit, FurCon 2020; interviews with various attendees; https://www.furtherconfusion.org/=

Forging Ahead

Site visit and interview with Yori Seeger.

Secondhand Chic

Site visit; interview with Stephen Borasi, Vice President of Retail, Goodwill of Silicon Valley, February 2020; https://www.mercurynews.com/2016/11/02/redesigned-goodwill-reopens-doors-unveils-upscale-boutique

Cowboys and Ice Cream

Site visit; *The Devil in Silicon Valley: Northern California, Race, and Mexican Americans* by Stephen J. Pitti; http://www.lostigresdelnorte.com/english/about.html

Raising the Dead

https://www.mercurynews.com/2015/11/30/grateful-dead-was-born-50-years-ago-in-san-jos/; https://ultimateclassicrock.com/grateful-dead-first-show; https://www.mercurynews.com/2008/06/29/historic-rock-landmarks-in-santa-clara-county; http://www.metroactive.com/features/columns/Silicon-Alleys-House-Inspired-Beat-Generation.html

Guided by Guilt?

Interview with Janan Boehme, Winchester Mystery House; *Captive of the Labyrinth: Sarah L. Winchester, Heiress to the Rifle Fortune* by Mary Jo Ignoffo

Sacred Secrets

Site visit; *Rosicrucian Manual* by H. Spencer Lewis; https://www.kqed.org/news/11551947/what-is-the-rosicrucian-egyptian-museum-and-why-is-it-in-san-jose

Truly Hartless

Swift Justice: Murder and Vengeance in a California Town by Harry Farrell; https://www.mercurynews.com/2017/09/24/san-joses-1933-lynching-a-guide-to-historic-sites; https://www.sanjose.org/listings/harts-dog-park

That's Electric

"The Light Between Two Towers" documentary: https://www.sanjoselighttower.com; http://historysanjose.org/wp/plan-your-visit/history-park/electric-light-tower; https://www.sjpl.org/blog/looking-back-san-joses-electric-light-tower; https://www.orlandosentinel.com/news/os-xpm-1989-12-30-8912303687-story.html; http://scbenchbar.com

Boom Town

https://www.mercurynews.com/2009/09/04/herhold-two-mckinley-statues-two-very-different-towns; http://www.scscourt.org/general_info/community/och_history.shtml; https://cdnc.ucr.edu/?a=d&d=LAH19180502.2.636&e=-------en--20--1--txt-txIN--------1

Criminal or Crusader?

Trailing the California Bandit: Tiburcio Vasquez by Ralph Rambo; "Downtown San Jose Mexican Historic Sites Tour": https://www.arcgis.com/apps/MapTour/index.html?appid=0d6902c1c17f4ca08658e446736a5432#map

Island Living

https://www.kqed.org/news/10953849/whats-it-like-to-live-in-an-urban-island; https://www.spur.org/publications/urbanist-article/2013-04-04/shaping-downtown-san-jose; Correspondence with Rob Eastwood, Santa Clara County Dept. of Planning & Development, July 2020; https://www.sccgov.org/sites/dpd/DocsForms/Documents/UrbanIslands_Atlas_2016.pdf

Howdy, Pardner

Site visit; video: "Lost Parks of Northern California: Frontier Village" https://greatamericanthrills.net/lost-parks/frontier-village

Five Chinatowns

Site visit; interview with Anita Wong Kwock, Chinese Historical & Cultural Project; *150 Years of Chinese Lives in the Santa Clara Valley* by Michael S. Chang; *San Jose Japantown: A Journey* by Curt Fukuda; https://www.npr.org/sections/codeswitch/2017/03/17/520517665/that-time-american-women-lost-their-citizenship-because-they-married-foreigners

Butterfly Effect
Site visit; interview with Joe Faria; *Capelinhos, A Volcano of Synergies: Azorean Emigration to America* by Tony Goulart.

Resist and Remember
https://www.jamsj.org; https://www.britannica.com/event/Japanese-American-internment

Pound for Pound
Interview with Ron Ogi; https://www.wesleysj.net/mochitsuki

Color y Cultura
Site visit; https://www.mercurynews.com/2018/12/16/san-joses-disappearing-murals-its-like-wiping-away-peoples-history; https://abc7news.com/society/historic-mural-de-la-raza-painted-over-in-san-jose-community-outraged/4115162; https://www.kqed.org/arts/13845793/walkabout-san-joses-chicano-murals

Community Kitchen
Site visits; interview with Sikh Gurdwara Sahib Board President, Bob Dhillon; http://www.sanjosegurdwara.org

Cinema and Chai
Site visit; https://www.towne3.com; *Swift Justice: Murder and Vengeance in a California Town* by Harry Farrell

Low and Slow
https://www.mercurynews.com/2015/06/24/san-jose-founder-and-writer-for-lowrider-magazine-has-died; https://www.latimes.com/entertainment-arts/story/2019-12-13/lowrider-magazine-ceases-print

Slip and Slide
Site visits; https://www.yelp.com/biz/brigadoon-park-san-jose

Sea Strikes
Site visit; *100 Things to Do in San Jose Before You Die* by Susannah Greenwood; https://www.unclebucksfishbowlandgrill.com

Speed City
African Americans of San Jose and Santa Clara County by Jan Batiste Adkins; https://www.kqed.org/news/11699649/50-years-on-the-olympic-power-salute-of-1968-gets-its-due-respect; https://theundefeated.com/features/san-jose-state-to-revive-its-fabled-speed-city-track-program

Chomp Champions
https://www.mercurynews.com/2017/07/01/san-joses-speed-eating-champs-joey-chestnut-and-matt-stonie-who-are-these-guys; https://www.mattstonie.com; https://majorleagueeating.com

Round About
Site visit; interview with Bess Hernandez-Jones; https://hellyervelodrome.com

On Thin Ice
Site visit; http://www.solar4americaiceatsanjose.com/

Krazy George
https://www.espn.com/blog/playbook/fandom/post/_/id/18888/its-settled-where-the-wave-first-started; https://www.youtube.com/watch?v=QQ9qgx74OL8; https://abc7news.com/5629902

Rocking Out
https://www.kqed.org/quest/42715/stanfords-signature-sandstone

Public Defender
Woman Lawyer: The Trials of Clara Foltz by Barbara Babcock; http://www.scscourt.org/general_info/community/och_history.shtml

In Storage
https://ethw.org/Milestones:RAMAC,_1956; https://www.macworld.com/article/1156757/computerhistorymuseum.html; https://www.computerhistory.org/storageengine/first-commercial-hard-disk-drive-shipped

On the Air
Site visit; http://perhamcollection.historysanjose.org/people-companies/charles-doc-herrold; https://www.charlesherrold.org/know.html

Behind the Vines
Site visit; interview with Amelia Littleton, JAM PR for J. Lohr, Oct. 2019; https://www.brewerygems.com/wieland.htm; http://a-falstaff-collector.com/Breweries/falstaffplant6,s.html; https://www.kqed.org/news/10695652/non-natives-in-california-snails-humans-and-other-species; https://www.almaden.com/about-us/; http://fowca.blogspot.com/2009/11/almaden-winery.html

Cutting 'Cots
Site visit; http://onlineexhibits.historysanjose.org/cannerylife/index.html; *Santa Clara County: Harvest of Change* by Stephen M. Payne.

Bearded Beauties
Site visit and interview with Nola Prevost; *100 Things to Do in San Jose Before You Die* by Susannah Greenwood

Swarm Site
Site visit; https://www.atlasobscura.com/places/first-honey-bees-in-california; https://www.losangelescountybeekeepers.com/history-of-honey-bees-in-ameri; https://www.agclassroom.org/teacher/stats/california.pdf

Varied Veggies
Interview with Raul Lozano, 2018; https://www.valleyverde.org

What a Treat
Site visit; https://www.chowhound.com/food-news/196611/this-hidden-san-jose-ice-cream-factory-is-a-treat-literally; http://historysanjose.org/wp/plan-your-visit/history-park/museum-store-cafe

No Waffling
Site visit; Email exchange with Kellogg Media Relations, October 2019; https://www.nytimes.com/1996/01/20/us/frank-dorsa-88-waffle-developer.html

Cheesy Fun
Site visit; https://www.fastcompany.com/40425172/robots-pizza-and-magic-the-chuck-e-cheese-origin-story

Scorned Love
The Love Life of Brigadier General Henry M. Naglee by Mary L. Schell; https://www.ttownmedia.com/tracy_press/archives/tracing-tracy-territory-man-who-began-tracy-s-water-legacy/article_e2a7c4d7-1ef3-5b88-99b1-7704603a27ae.html; *150 Years of Chinese Lives in the Santa Clara Valley* by Michael S. Chang

Hot Stuff

Site visit; https://www.huffpost.com/entry/topless-baristas_n_956098; https://www.mercurynews.com/2011/06/19/san-joses-vietnamese-cafes-serving-up-coffee-tea-and-whee; Yelp search for "vietnamese cafes" near San Jose

Supremely Delicious

http://www.godsdirectcontact.org/spiritualpractice/Master_Ching_Hai.htm; https://www.phoenixnewtimes.com/news/critics-claim-supreme-master-ching-hais-followers-restaurants-featuring-tasty-vegan-fare-front-for-an-exploitive-movement-6449095

Painted Ladies

Site visit; https://www.sourdougheatery.com/index.html; http://www.metroactive.com/papers/metro/12.09.99/alacarte-9949.html

Main Squeeze

Site visit; https://www.latimes.com/archives/la-xpm-2010-mar-03-la-me-orange-stands3-2010mar03-story.html; https://abc7news.com/5373792; http://www.weirdca.com/location.php?location=134; https://www.mercurynews.com/2010/04/16/pizarro-marks-hot-dogs-gets-new-owners-mini-makeover

Pup Party

Site visit; correspondence with Judy Conner; http://www.barksanjose.org

First in Flight

https://www.evergreenmuralwalk.com/2016/05/09/john-j-montgomery-aviating-pioneer; https://www.nbcbayarea.com/news/local/who-was-really-first-in-flight/1937617

Just My Type

Site visit and interview with Jim Gard, San Jose Printers' Guild; https://printersguild.wordpress.com

The Earliest EVs

Site visit; http://historysanjose.org/wp/plan-your-visit/history-park/trolley-barn; https://www.spur.org/publications/urbanist-article/2013-04-04/shaping-downtown-san-jose

Springs Eternal

Site visit; *Cultural and Natural History of Alum Rock Park* by R.J. Hartesveldt and H.T. Harvey; https://www.kqed.org/quest/15145/alum-rock-exploration; https://calisphere.org/item/ark:/13030/kt6h4nc6r0

Ancient Giants

https://www.parks.ca.gov/?page_id=540; https://sempervirens.org/about-us/our-history

I'm with the Band

Interview with Josh Scullen, February 2020; https://www.sfbbo.org; *Santa Clara County: Harvest of Change* by Stephen M. Payne

Wave of the Future

Treatment plant tour, February 2020; https://www.purewater4u.org

Drowned Town

Amtrak trip, San Jose to Oakland; https://www.mercurynews.com/2018/07/17/how-drawbridge-is-drowning-and-what-it-means-for-our-future; https://www.kqed.org/news/11549263/the-island-ghost-town-in-the-middle-of-san-francisco-bay

Losing Ground

https://scv-habitatagency.org/; https://vimeo.com/325789835/1e87ccd7dc; https://www.sfbbo.org/habitat-loss.html

Lost Lakes

https://www.sfei.org/sites/default/files/biblio_files/CoyoteCreek_HistoricalEcology_
SFEI_2006.pdf; https://news.openspaceauthority.org/blog/saving-san-joses-largest-
remaining-wetland

A Heavenly Site

Site visit; "Stories of Mount Umunhum" video: https://www.openspace.org/mount-
umunhum-sierra-azul; https://www.mercurynews.com/2019/12/06/2-4-million-in-
repairs-approved-for-landmark-mount-umunhum-radar-tower

Hicks Road

Site visit; conversations with local friends; http://searchlightsj.com/2015/hicks-road-
haunted-or-hyped

Paranormal Prowl

"Ghosts & History Walk of Downtown San Jose, October 2019" by Bay Area Ghost Hunters;
https://www.meetup.com/Bay-Area-Ghost-Hunters

Donner Destiny

https://www.nationalgeographic.com/news/2017/06/donner-party-cannibalism-nation-
west/; https://www.mercurynews.com/2016/08/01/why-new-san-jose-apartments-
have-a-donner-party-plaque

The Fearless Geers

http://www3.sanjoseca.gov/clerk/Agenda/20120605/20120605_0401.pdf; http://
historysanjose.org/wp/research-collection/frances-dainty-co-collection/; http://www.
metroactive.com/papers/metro/09.28.05/history-0539.html

Tryin' to Be Good

https://www.mercurynews.com/2010/09/01/roadshow-rotten-robbie-founder-herb-
richards-dies-at-98/; https://www.rottenrobbie.com/about-us/; https://cstoredecisions.
com/2016/02/29/how-rotten-robbie-got-ready-to-grow

California Modern

Site visit; https://www.mercurynews.com/2019/08/14/eichler-neighborhood-in-san-jose-
added-to-historic-register; Gale, Roy (1958-06-28). "Jim Crow Real Estate Men Hit by
Calif. Court" https://www.themilitant.com/1958/2227/MIL2227.pdf, https://ohp.parks.
ca.gov/pages/1067/files/CA_Santa%20Clara_San%20Jose%20Housing%20Tracts%20
of%20Joseph%20Eichler%20MPD_Fairglen%20Additions_DRAFT.pdf

Stitched Together

Site visit; https://www.sjquiltmuseum.org; https://sjmqt.tumblr.com; https://www.
mercurynews.com/2018/07/04/quilt-museum-takes-aim-at-gun-violence

Get Lit

The San Jose Signs Project: A Guide to the Vintage Signage of San Jose by Heather David

INDEX